Defining a Nation

REACTING TO THE PAST is an award-winning series of immersive role-playing games that actively engage students in their own learning. Students assume the roles of historical characters and practice critical thinking, primary source analysis, and argument, both written and spoken. Reacting games are flexible enough to be used across the curriculum, from first-year general education classes and discussion sections of lecture classes to capstone experiences, intersession courses, and honors programs.

Reacting to the Past was originally developed under the auspices of Barnard College and is sustained by the Reacting Consortium of colleges and universities. The Consortium hosts a regular series of conferences and events to support faculty and administrators.

Note to instructors: Before beginning the game you must download the Gamemaster's Materials, including an instructor's guide containing a detailed schedule of class sessions, role sheets for students, and handouts.

To download this essential resource, visit https://reactingconsortium.org/games, click on the page for this title, then click "Instructors Guide."

Defining a Nation
India on the Eve of Independence, 1945

Ainslie T. Embree and Mark C. Carnes

REACTING
TO THE PAST

BARNARD

The University of North Carolina Press

Chapel Hill

The University of North Carolina Press has been a member of the
Green Press Initiative since 2003.

Cover illustration: Mahatma Gandhi en route to see the Indian viceroy at Simla,
Himachal Pradesh, India, June 23, 1945. Dinodia Photos / Alamy Stock Photo

ISBN 978-1-4696-7079-9 (pbk.: alk. paper)
ISBN 978-1-4696-7229-8 (e-book)

DEDICATION: To Fiza Quraishi, whose spunk, creativity, and leadership helped conceive of Reacting to the Past.

CONTENTS

The Train to Simla, June 1945

Through the train's window, smeared with grit and soot, you ponder the torrent of people surging along the station platform. Why, you wonder, do the British recoil from the swirling masses of India? You delight in the profusion of humanity, the sea of people in the station: The black-turbaned Sikh, with a long brown beard. Three dark children, begging for food. A Muslim swathed in clothing, her eyes darting through the slits. A young Hindu prince in a Savile Row linen suit. A university student in white homespun cotton—*khadi*—Gandhi's emblem of Indian independence. Sprinkled here and there, British soldiers in khaki, walking with that brisk, purposeful swagger that won an empire—and may soon lose it.

So many people! The numbers spin in your head: 400 million in all. 300 million Hindus. 100 million Muslims. Millions more Sikhs, Pashtuns, Parsees, Christians, Jews. Many are desperately needy: 60 million Untouchables, among them the barefoot children whose eyes, penetrating the grime of the window, match your stare. They run towards you, arms raised, hands outstretched. You tug at the window to lower it, but it is stuck. You stand, fumbling in your pocket for coins, and try to pry the window open. Just as it begins to loosen, a man outside in a blue uniform scurries toward the children and shoos them away. One looks back at you beseechingly.

Her face says it all. She needs you. They all need you. That is your task at Simla. You must create a new government—a government of and by the Indian people. But can the Indians come together to build a new India? And if a united India is impossible, as Jinnah and the Muslim League claim, can multiple nations be carved out of the subcontinent? And what of the vulnerable minorities, such as these "Untouchable" children? If you fail, if the plans to make a new government collapse, what will happen to them?

Alone in the compartment, you look at your watch, a gift from your father. He was proud of you for graduating near the top of your class. It was a British-style school, with desks in neat rows, and where everything was measured in time. Where you learned English, and how to sing "God Save the King," and how to hold a bat and bowl a googly.

The train should have left thirty minutes ago, before the summer sun bakes the Ganges plains. But the war has shredded train schedules. Locomotives and passenger cars have been diverted to send fresh troops to Burma and to bring the wounded back from the front. But soon it will be over. Soon Japan will surrender, their attempt to invade India a failure.

Britain apparently didn't need India's help after all. Maybe Gandhi had been right, back in 1942, when he refused to support the British war effort against Japan and instead demanded that the British "Quit India." When the British refused, Gandhi and the Indian National Congress intensified their protests for independence—and nearly all of the INC leaders ended up in British prisons during the war. But now they have been released, and invited to Simla, the summer capital of British India.

Like most Indian leaders, you have spent much of your life in British boxes. Either in prisons, for challenging British rule—or on trains, hurrying from one town to another, giving speeches and meeting organizers. Nearly always you speak to each other in English—not Marathi, Bengali, Gujarati, Punjabi, or any of the other local languages of the Indian people. That's the greatest irony. Britain has provided the implements for a modern nation—its railroads, bridges, laws, governmental structures, and common language, all of which Indian nationalists are utilizing in the fight for independence.

A thought occurs to you: Gandhi, too, has doubtless been summoned to Simla. Is he on this train? Though he denounces trains as a symbol of the soulless modern world, he has little choice but to take them. It is one thing to walk several hundred miles on the "Salt March" to the sea, to protest the British salt monopoly. Though it occurred fifteen years ago, back in 1930, you will never forget it. You recall his slow walk, leaning on a bamboo cane, stopping at hundreds of villages along the way. Huge crowds followed, and the eyes of the world watched. Weeks stretched into months. When he finally crossed the beach to the sea, he declared: "Watch, I am about to give a signal to the nation." Then he leaned over, scooped a handful of salt, and lifted it up—an offering for the multitude. The crowd, now numbering in the tens of thousands, surged across the beach and dipped pans and pails into the salt deposits. The British responded with stupid brutality, arresting hundreds and then thousands of his followers. Protests erupted throughout India. Perhaps 100,000 were imprisoned. A pinch of salt, sprinkled into the winds, and so falls an empire!

But you realize that Gandhi will not be on this train. Even a rumor of his arrival would swamp the station with thousands seeking a glimpse of the "great soul"—the *Mahatma*—the conscience of India. And of course he would not be riding with you. He would never travel first class. You reproach yourself for this small luxury. You must use this long train ride to review your notes and prepare your speech. You must find the right path and persuade the British governors—and the other Indian leaders—to take it.

You again look at your watch, and examine the train schedule. Then you notice a commotion on the platform. Is it Gandhi, after all? Then you spot a handful of British soldiers running toward your train. An Indian conductor puts his hands out, and then moves to block their way. The first soldier, with a thin black mustache, waves a slip of paper at him. The conductor, glancing at the paper, shakes his head. Yours is a first-class compartment, more than is allowed for regular soldiers. A sandy-haired soldier smiles at the conductor, makes a small bow, and gently pushes past the conductor and jogs toward the train. The others follow close behind, and clamber up the steps to your car. You gather your papers and put them into a briefcase. A few seconds later, the door to your compartment opens. The sandy-haired soldier, his captain's tunic drenched in sweat, peers in and asks:

"Excuse me, but do you mind if we join you?"

You hesitate—you have important work to do—but then nod. "Please," you say, gesturing to the three seats opposite you.

The captain sits across from you by the window, and the others sit next to him. Outside, the conductor is gesturing angrily toward the train and calling to others. Across from you, the soldiers exchange looks, and laugh.

A few minutes later you hear a *thunk* below your feet as the gears of the train engage. Soon it jerks forward. This is one of the older trains, destined for scrap long ago but forced into service because of the war. You wonder whether it will manage the long climb into the mountains.

"So as I was saying, I saw the bunker where they found Hitler. Him and Eva." This from the soldier with the mustache. He's speaking to the private to his right, a large man with enormous boots.

"Said to meself, 'War's over.' Thought I'd soon be havin' a pint at the Black Horse. Now look at me. I end up in bloody 'ell." Bigfoot laughs.

"You think this is bad?" the captain says, looking at the others. "You could be chasing the Japanese through Indochina. This job is a vacation."

"He's right," Bigfoot says. "The Japs shoot back." "Over here, with Gandhi's crowd, you hit 'em on the head, and they say, 'Why, thankee very much, gov'ner. Punch me stomach when you get a chance.'" More chuckles, though the captain fleetingly glances at you. Then he looks out the window.

The train crawls through the congested old city of Delhi, passing the crumbling walls that had been built centuries ago. Many of the stones have been scavenged for huts and hovels for Untouchables, who have been shunted to the outskirts.

Then to the right, beyond several warehouses, you see the immense pink mass of the Red Fort, the capital of the Mughal Empire and home of the royal family during the seventeenth century. When you were a schoolboy, your history teacher, speaking in halting English, had explained that the fort had been the site of the climactic battle of the "Sepoy Mutiny" in 1857. Back then, India was ruled by the British East India Company, which hired Indians to serve as soldiers. That year, thousands had rebelled against the British, seizing several cities in northern India, and proclaiming Bahadur Shah, a descendent of the great Mughal emperors, to be the new ruler of India. As the rebellion collapsed, many Indian soldiers took refuge in the Red Fort. When captured, some had been strapped to cannon and summarily executed; Bahudar Shah was convicted of mass murder and exiled.

Your teacher, following the British interpretation, had referred to it as the "Sepoy Mutiny"—an act of illegal treachery; but your briefcase contains Savarkar's history of what he called the "great rebellion" against the British—the first battle in the long war for Hindu independence. Probably Savarkar is making plans for the final battle in the coming months. Savarkar's book has long been banned as seditious. You had misgivings about bringing it to Simla, where doubtless your bags will be searched by military police. But your edition of the book is in Bengali, which few Brits have troubled to learn.

Then it dawns on you. Has Savarkar been invited to Simla, too? What delicious irony: A convicted Hindu terrorist, who languished for years in a British prison in the Indian Ocean, now being housed as a guest of the Viceroy! Amazing times, indeed!

The train gains speed as it heads north across the plains. You open your briefcase, bulging with papers: treaties, population studies, reports on geographical and economic resources, and newspapers in many different languages. Soon you are dozing.

A jolt—a bomb! Instantly you're on your feet. You trip over the boots of Bigfoot. "Bloody 'ell," he mutters. In an instant it's over. There was no bomb. But it had been right along this section of track, over a decade ago. You had seen the blackened train. Everyone was amazed that Viceroy Irwin had walked away, unhurt. "It was a miracle," the Anglican priest said in the ceremony of thanksgiving afterwards. The bomb-thrower had also escaped. Many suspected he had been with Savarkar.

"I beg your pardon," you tell Bigfoot.

He looks up at you and stares. Then he glances at Mustache, and shakes his head. Mustache whispers something, covering his mouth. Bigfoot smiles.

You sit back down.

The train slows. "Panipat Station," the conductor shouts, and then repeats the words in Punjabi. Two of the British soldiers leave the compartment. Now they're approaching a Muslim vendor. A few minutes later they return, and offer their captain some paratta rolls. He shakes his head. "You're not supposed to bring food in here."

"It's long past noon," Mustache notes.

"There is a dining room," the captain replies.

"Don't take army chits for that, now, do they?" Mustache adds. Then he looks at you, and, without breaking his stare, takes a bite of his roll.

You shake your head and Mustache takes a huge bite.

"Good God, man, look at the mess you're making," the captain says.

"Made a bigger mess on the train after taking a bullet at Imphal now, didn't I? Protecting these sodding black bastards" Mustache says, his eyes still fixed on you.

"That's enough," the captain says.

"You and your bleedin' wound," Bigfoot mutters. "I've seen more blood shaving my face."

You focus on your papers.

Soon the train is moving again. Though furious with Mustache, you resolve to move past it, and so you study the scenery. Perhaps there is no place on earth richer in history, though none of it is marked with monuments. Somewhere out there is the "the field of truth" at Panipat—from the opening lines of the *Bhagavad Gita,* the classic Hindu text. The *Gita* begins when two great clans—the Pandavas and the Kauravas—line up to fight a great battle. Arjuna, a Pandava warrior, agonizes over the prospect of killing his cousins, so he orders his charioteer, Krishna, to drive to a vantage point between the two armies. What follows is a meditation on destiny and *dharma*— one's assigned social role—that culminates in Krishna revealing himself to be merely a human manifestation of the cosmic light of the universe. And it occurred right out there!—or so the legend goes.

In addition to this mythic battle was a real one. It also occurred at Panipat: this time, your teacher had explained, in 1526 when Babar, the first Mughal king, defeated the Afghan potentate who then ruled northern India. This was the beginning of rule by the Mughal Muslims. Then Akbar, the greatest Mughal ruler, won another pivotal battle at Panipat. And others still later.

Panipat is the fulcrum of all India. To your left—the west—lies the rich farmland that stretches to the Punjab and beyond. All the rivers on that side of the train flow to the west, through the arid high country of the Punjab. Then the western rivers merge with the Indus and pour into the Arabian Sea. To the right—the Jumna River gleams in the late afternoon sun. The Jumna originates high in the Himalayas, its waters nourished by the tears of Shiva, a Hindu deity. Then it flows into the Ganges and empties into the Bay of Bengal. Two different rivers, two different peoples.

A knock on your cabin door. The Indian steward pushes open the door to the compartment and brings in tea and biscuits. He bows slightly to each of the soldiers in turn, who take a handful of biscuits and tea, and then to you. Then he departs. The compartment is too warm, and so you stand up and pull at the window, which sticks momentarily, and then bangs down.

You breathe in the rich smell of cow dung—the perfect fuel and fertilizer. Soon you see a herd of cattle grazing by the river. To you, the cow is life: a giver of essential nutrients, a universal expression of mother-force and thus of life itself. Some Hindus insist that Indian independence will bring an end to the slaughter of cows by Muslims, who eat beef. Your briefcase contains a fat folder on the Cow Protection Movement.

The British soldiers, who had been dozing, begin to stir.

"Good God, this whole fucking place stinks," Mustache declares.

"All India is one big joke," says Bigfoot. "It'll last about as long as the gin in this flask." He reaches into his coat pocket and takes a swig. He passes it to Mustache, and then to the captain, both of whom lift the bottle to their lips and drink deeply.

"How they going to be a nation if they don't even defend themselves?" Mustache asks. "They tell us to 'get out,' but if we 'ad, Gandhi'd be wearing a kimono instead of that diaper."

"Wish he were," Bigfoot says. "I can smell the diaper. Right outside that window."

The laughter turns raucous.

"What a nation!" Mustache adds, words slurred.

"Led by a man who gives speeches in his underwear," Bigfoot continues.

"Excuse me," you say, leaning toward the captain. "You must know that consumption of alcohol by soldiers on trains is forbidden."

He stares at you. The others fall silent.

"We're on leave," the captain says, eyes narrowing. "From fighting the Japs."

"That makes no difference," you say. "Army regulations. Section 4, article 10, I believe."

"You sure about that?" he asks.

"Yes, I am," you say, "though we can check with the adjutant at the next station. And we can ask about your traveling in a first-class compartment." You look at him steadily, though you know nothing about British army regulations.

"I'm an officer," he says. "I have a chit."

"But they aren't," you say, nodding toward the others. "And they don't."

He fixes you with a hard stare. "This compartment was empty."

"I beg to differ," you say, looking him in the eye. Then you reach down, take hold of your briefcase, put it on your lap, and arrange your papers. Then you pull out a folder and pretend to read it. Your heart is racing.

The officer leans forward, as if to speak, and then he turns to the others. "Put the bleeding flask away," he growls.

The room falls silent. You feel their eyes upon you. You jot some notes on a report. The train slows to a stop. No one seems to depart or get on, and then the train resumes its journey. Within a few hours it will begin its torturous, twisting climb through the foothills of the Himalayas; by the end of the day it will be winding around steep mountains toward Simla, the British summer capital.

India's climb to nationhood, too, will be a difficult one. The ultimate destination—at Simla—is nationhood. But the grade is steep, and the obstacles many. And if the train lurches off the track, many will die.

Introduction

WHAT IS A NATION?

Is it a people who share common values, such as the Chinese of the Ming Dynasty, steeped in Confucianism, or the Israelites, who followed laws put forth by their God? Is a nation a geographical entity, such as the city-states of ancient Greece or the peoples encompassed by the Spanish Empire? Is a nation a form of contract, where people agree to come together to achieve something greater than what they could accomplish individually, such as the republic embodied by the Constitution of the United States? Is a nation an expression of racial identity, such as seventeenth-century Japan or white South Africa during much of the twentieth century? Is a nation a people who share a religious vision, such as the Catholics of France during the seventeenth century or Sunni Arabs today? Or is national identity itself an outmoded concept, as might be believed by people who think of themselves as members of the European Union or, more broadly, as "global citizens"?

This game seeks to answer these questions as they apply to the Indian subcontinent after World War II. More, the game raises the question of how various notions of nationhood are applied in the creation of new states. Few issues are more salient to our own times. During the seven decades since World War II much of the world has undergone upheaval. Old governmental systems have collapsed and new ones have emerged—and are still emerging. The fate of colonial India prefigures the shape of the modern world.

This game begins in June 1945. World War II is drawing to a close. Nazi Germany surrendered the previous month. Japan's empire in the Pacific has collapsed, and Americans are making plans to invade Okinawa in preparation for the eventual conquest of Japan. The Soviet Union, governed by a communist hierarchy led by the formidable Josef Stalin, has filled the vacuum in Eastern Europe caused by the collapse of Nazi Germany. Many expect that communism will spread through war-ravaged Western Europe. Many, too, expect that in the wake of the inevitable withdrawal of the Japanese army, China will descend into chaos with the resumption of the civil war between the communist forces of Mao Zedong and those of nationalist leader Chiang Kai-shek. There is talk of a new League of Nations, a "United Nations," but few think that any such international organization will be capable of ensuring peace and stability.

Nowhere is the situation more confused than in India. Great Britain is emerging from the war victorious, but its economy has been crippled. Whether it can retain India, the "jewel in the crown" of British imperialism, is doubtful. Prime Minister Winston Churchill, Britain's leader during the war and an ardent advocate of British imperialism, is losing public support. Within India, protests against colonial rule have intensified throughout the twentieth century, and the emergence of Mohandas Gandhi has energized Indian politics as never before. Gandhi has combined a vision of Indian independence with a new means of attaining it: nonviolent civil disobedience.

In 1942 Gandhi asserted his power with tremendous force. At the time, the Japanese army had swarmed over Southeast Asia and was advancing through Burma into India. Britain called on Indian leaders to support the war against Japan and Germany. In return for India's wholehearted support for the war, Britain offered to invite India to join the British Dominion as an equal member afterward. The Indian National Congress, which had spearheaded Indian nationalism since its inception in 1885, rejected this proposal outright. Gandhi likened it to "a blank cheque on a failing bank." Gandhi instead called on Indians to insist on immediate independence from Britain, even if it weakened the British war effort. "I have made up my mind that it would be a good thing if a million people were shot in a brave and nonviolent rebellion against the British rule," he declared. The Congress party endorsed his call for nonviolent protests against British rule through the "Quit India" movement.

The British viceroy outlawed the "Quit India" movement and arrested most of the leaders of the nationalist movement, including Gandhi. This ignited more riots and even a spate of attacks on railroad bridges and telegraph depots. Field Marshal Viscount Wavell arrived the next year to spearhead the defense of India from the Japanese. In 1944, Gandhi and Muslim secularist Ali Jinnah met to discuss the future of India: Gandhi insisted that India be a single nation, encompassing all faiths and peoples; Jinnah declared that India contained two separate states, one Hindu, the other Muslim. The talks went nowhere.

Three months ago (March 1945), as the Japanese threat receded, Wavell went to London to confer with the Foreign Ministry and Prime Minister Churchill. He returned several weeks ago. On June 14, he announced in a radio broadcast his plans to convene at Simla an executive council of Indian political leaders to discuss the fate of the subcontinent. The next day, he ordered that imprisoned Congress officials be released.

Churchill, an ardent imperialist, has made noises about retaining some form of British rule or influence over India, but this appears unlikely. During the war, the United States pressured Great Britain to allow colonial peoples the right to self-determination after the war, a principle that was encompassed in the Atlantic Charter. Britain signed the document, as did all the Allies. Whether they would fulfill the provisions of the Charter now that Germany had surrendered remained unclear. Apart from Britain's legal obligation to retreat from colonial domination, there is the painful economic fact that Britain has been nearly bankrupted by the war. It now lacks the resources and perhaps the will to impose its rule on 400 million Indians.

What, then, will become of India?

India: Chronology

POPULATION (APPROXIMATE)

300 BCE	100 million
1700	100 million
1800	125 million
1871	250 million: 187 Hindu, 52 Muslim
1940	400 million: 300 Hindu, 100 Muslim

PRINCIPAL EVENTS

1500s	Spread of Sikh faith (founded by Nanak [1469–1538])
1526–1761	Mughal Empire
1526	Babar defeats Afghan king, establishes Mughal (Muslim) dynasty
1556	Akbar consolidates and expands empire
1658	Aurangzeb rules to 1707
1676	Aurangzeb executes Teg Bahadur, leader of Sikhs, and ignites rebellion
1685	Shivaji, Hindu warlord, establishes Maratha kingdom in south
1708	Govind Singh (1666–1708), Sikh leader, establishes militant order
1717	British East India Company secures favorable trading rights from Mughals; expands influence and power
1757	East India Company seizes Calcutta and much of Bengal
1763	Treaty of Paris, ending the "Great War for the Empire," leaves British East India Company dominant in India
1857	Indian upheaval ("Sepoy Mutiny") crushed
1858	Government of India Act: Britain rules India as a crown colony
1878	Viceroy Lytton's Vernacular Press Act suppresses Indian opposition
1882	Chatterji's novel, *Anandamath,* incites opposition to British in Bengal
1885	Indian National Congress (INC) founded
1905	Viceroy Curzon proposes partition of Bengal
1906	Muslim League founded
1914	Europe engulfed in Great War; Indian leaders endorse British war effort
1916	Muslim League (Jinnah) and INC agree on provincial power (Lucknow Pact)
1917	British adopt dyarchy: shared power with Indian leaders at provincial level
1918	Armistice ends the Great War
1919	Britain imposes repressive laws (Rowlatt Acts); protests ensue Amritsar massacre leaves 400 dead
1920	Khilafat Movement: Protests over demise of (Muslim) caliphate in Turkey
1921–1922	Gandhi leads noncooperation protests; suspended after killings at Chauri Chaura
1930	Gandhi leads salt march civil disobedience; Iqbal, Muslim writer, calls for separate Muslim state
1932	Gandhi, protesting British offer of separate legislative seats for Untouchables, goes on hunger strike; Ambedkar rescinds demand for separate electorates for Untouchables (Poona Pact)

1935	Government of India Act provides for election of provincial legislators, with some seats reserved for minorities
1937	INC, despite promises to boycott the election, wins majority in most provinces
1940	Germany invades France, crushes French and British armies; Churchill seeks Indian support (Cripps Mission, 1941)
1942	Gandhi and INC reject Cripps, demand Britain "Quit India"; Congress leaders arrested
1945	Germany surrenders (May); Japanese forces routed

Maps

MAP A. BRITISH INDIA C. 1930

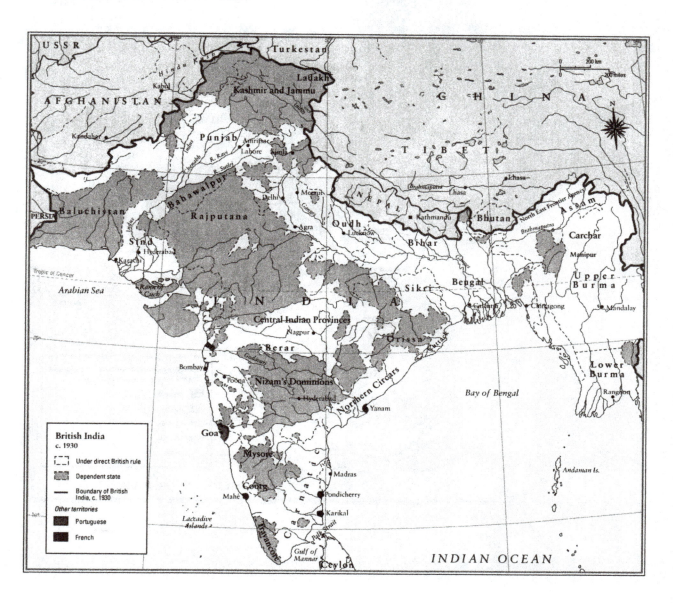

MAP B. MUSLIMS AS PERCENT OF TOTAL POPULATION C. 1930

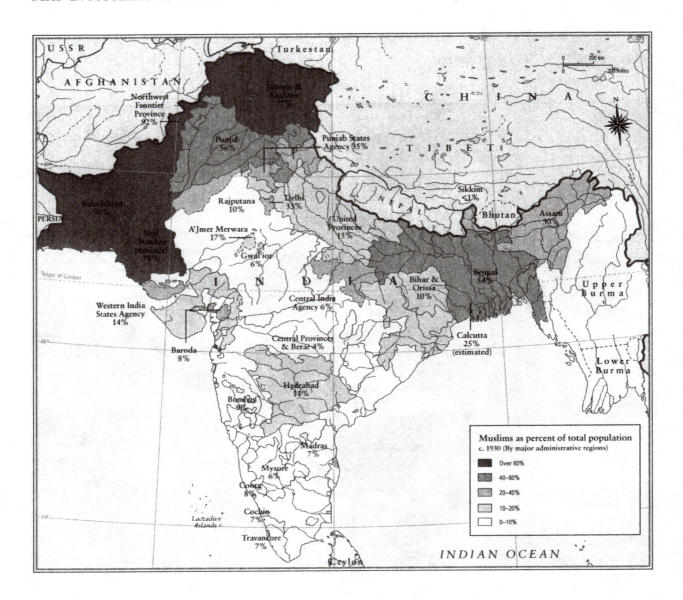

Muslims as percent of total population
c. 1930 (By major administrative regions)

Over 60%
40–60%
20–40%
10–20%
0–10%

Defining a Nation: India on the Eve of Independence, 1945

Unfinished Journey: From the Mughals to the British Raj and Beyond

INDIA UNDER THE MUGHALS: 1500–1700

The plains of northern India, whose rivers are fed by the melting snows of the Himalayas, have long been among the most fertile agricultural regions in the world. Several of the earliest civilizations have grown up along the shores of the Ganges and Indus Rivers; and for thousands of years Indian peoples have cultivated their fertile plains and deltas, gradually moving into the hill country in the north and the Deccan plateau in the south.

The early history of South Asia bears similarity to that of predominantly farming peoples throughout Asia, Africa, and Europe. Nearly everywhere, local warlords seized land, imposed taxes on the cultivators, and sought to conquer ever larger domains. The most successful warriors established hereditary dynasties. Much of premodern history—in India and elsewhere—chronicles the rise and fall of such kingdoms.

Some historians believe that Indian history entered its early modern phase in 1526, when the armies of Zahir al-Din Muhammad Babar (1483–1530) crushed those of an Afghan ruler at Panipat, northwest of Delhi. Although Babar ruled only four years, his victory laid the foundations of the Mughal dynasty, which would long dominate much of the Indian subcontinent. The pivotal figure in this transformation was Akbar, Babar's grandson, who defeated one after another regional rulers: Akbar's conquests extended the Mughal dynasty north to Kabul and Kashmir; east to Bengal; and south to the Arabian Sea and the Deccan plateau.

The ruling families of the Mughal dynasty were Muslim; and Akbar's conquests contributed to the diffusion of the Islamic religion—and Persian and Turkic culture. But Akbar respected other religions and ideas. He established a policy—continued by subsequent Mughal rulers—of taking wives from among conquered royal families without obliging them to convert to Islam. He welcomed theologians of many different creeds to his court, including Hindu gurus, Jesuit priests, and Muslim scholars of all types.

Akbar also allowed defeated chieftains to remain in power, as long as they professed loyalty to him—and forwarded annual tax payments to the imperial treasury. Akbar further extended his dominion by assigning some conquered lands to favored soldiers. These *jagirdirs* did not own their domains in the manner of European noblemen; rather, *jagirdirs* were entitled to tax agricultural produce, as long as a set portion of those taxes flowed into the emperor's coffers.

But imperial officials and even local chieftains found it difficult to squeeze taxes from wily peasants and farmers. In many villages the details of tax assessment and collection fell to the local *zamindar*, usually a well-to-do farmer who extended credit to villagers in need—and often provided leadership as well. Some *zamindars* acquired considerable wealth—and power. In the central plateau of southern India, for example, each of the over 1,000 fortified towns and villages was governed by a local *zamindar.*

The Mughal Empire was thus a complicated patchwork of overlapping political obligations. Chieftains, *jagirdirs,* and *zamindars* exercised considerable independence at the local level; but when recalcitrant officials fell behind on their tax obligations, Mughal rulers swiftly dispatched large armies to collect the taxes—and punish local officials.

For most of the seventeenth century, the Mughal Empire imposed peace and stability on much of the subcontinent. Rural population increased. Cities grew and emerged as centers of culture. Lahore, Agra, and Delhi each approached 1 million inhabitants—this at a time when Boston, the largest city in British America, had only 6,700 people and London, about 600,000. By 1700, moreover, India had been drawn into global commerce, exporting fine textiles, gems, spices, and other commodities, and receiving precious metals and horses in return.

But by the final decades of the seventeenth century, during the long reign (1658–1707) of Emperor Aurangzeb, cracks appeared in the foundations of the empire. Some historians believe that Aurangzeb weakened the empire by imposing higher taxes upon Hindus and giving preference to Muslims for administrative positions—actions that alienated many Hindus. But other factors also destabilized Indian society. Because population levels were rising, the failure of crops and resultant famine struck with special force. Sometimes ambitious *zamindars* exploited rural discontent to stage revolts against the emperor. Sometimes, too, entire regions revolted.

One of these revolts emerged in the Punjab, west of Delhi. By the late 1600s the Punjab was becoming a center for Sikhism, a religion based on the beliefs of Guru Nanak (1469–1539) as outlined in a sacred text called the *Guru Granth Sahib*. Nanak insisted that the divine resided in all human beings, and thus could be accessed through meditation and contemplation. Although Sikhism borrowed ideas from Islam and Hinduism, it often found itself at odds with both. The Sikh emphasis on personal meditation undermined the role of Brahmans, Hindu priests who presided over local rites and sacrifices; and the insistence that god was within every person contravened the Islamic concept of Allah. In 1676 Aurangzeb executed Tegh Bahadur, religious leader of the Sikhs, for blasphemy against Islam. Many Sikhs vowed vengeance, and encouraged male believers to enlist as soldier-saints in defense of the faith; some rebelled against Mughal rule in the Punjab.

But the most serious challenge to Aurangzeb came from Shivaji Bonsle (1630–80), a Hindu prince who belonged to the Maratha clan in southern India. Shivaji attracted followers by exploiting rural discontent and Hindu grievances against the Muslim dynasty. Then he built a series of forts in the hill country of southern India. When Aurangzeb sent armies to crush the forts, Shivaji ambushed the attackers. By 1685 Shivaji had established a Maratha kingdom in much of southern India.

When Aurangzeb died in 1707, the Mughal dynasty was in trouble. Afghan and Persian kings were making incursions in the north. Within India, ambitious *zamindars,* attempting to replicate Shivaji's earlier success, were founding their own kingdoms. *Jagirdirs,* frustrated by the failure of Aurangzeb's military ventures and craving more land allotments, withheld payments to the emperor. Pirates and criminal gangs plundered villages and claimed entire cities. Large clans or religious sects took control of vast regions—the Marathas in the Deccan; Sikhs in the Punjab; and Rajputs in Rajasthan. And many princes, having previously professed loyalty to the Mughal dynasty, reestablished their own kingdoms.

RISE OF THE BRITISH EAST INDIA COMPANY

As regional rulers were asserting their independence from Mughal rule, yet another factor destabilized the Mughal Empire: the British East India Company. Founded in 1600 and chartered by Queen Elizabeth, the British East India Company was a joint-stock venture that sought to exploit the fabled wealth of India. The company successfully petitioned the Mughal emperor to be allowed to enter into trade in India.

The British East India Company, though conceived as a profitable enterprise, held the promise of projecting British influence into southern Asia. In this sense it was similar to other English mercantile ventures—such as the various English joint-stock companies that founded colonies in Virginia and Massachusetts—which served as footholds for establishing British power in the Americas.

The East India Company established trading offices and built docks and warehouses in the main coastal cities. British merchants traded silver and copper for Asian spices, gems, fine textiles, tea, and saltpeter (used in the manufacture of gunpowder). The trade generated huge profits.

But the decline of the Mughal Empire disrupted trade. Some raiders—including Shivaji—attacked and looted the company's warehouses. Company officials hired soldiers to defend company property; then they built forts to protect company facilities in Bombay, Madras, and Calcutta. Mughal rulers rightly regarded these forts as challenges to their authority, but were powerless to shut them down.

That's because the British East India Company also brought a new form of warfare to India. Since the 1400s, European kings had been at war almost incessantly; their desperate struggles produced a formidable type of warfare. Skilled metalworkers learned how to cast metals into cannons capable of containing powerful gunpowder charges, which propelled heavy iron balls at high velocities. Such cannons could obliterate in a few days, or even hours, stone walls and fortifications that had stood for centuries. European rulers learned to mount cannons upon carriages drawn by horses, and upon large sailing vessels. This enabled them to wage war, and acquire power, against distant enemies. The introduction of this type of warfare to India further weakened the Mughals.

By the mid-1700s, Dutch and French merchants had established similar trading footholds in Indian port cities; and soon the race was on to determine which European company—and which European nation—would control the India trade. This issue was largely resolved in the 1750s during the Great War for the Empire, when British and French armies and navies fought from North America to the Indian Ocean. Britain prevailed, driving France from North America—and from India.

Now the East India Company focused on gaining control of India. By 1757 it had seized much of Bengal, the rich agricultural lower basin of the Ganges. By 1800, much of southern India had fallen under its domination as well. In the 1840s the British defeated the Sikhs and acquired much of the Punjab, completing the East India Company's domination of India. Like the Mughal rulers before them, company officials often allowed local princes, especially in the less valuable upland farming regions, to remain in power. The resultant treaties required the East India Company to provide military protection for the princely state; in return, the prince agreed to accept the guidance of a company official (a "Resident") and pay for the cost of the company's military protection.

THE "SEPOY MUTINY" (1858) AND THE RISE OF THE BRITISH RAJ

But in many localities tensions smoldered. Muslim elites were dismayed by the ascendancy of British officials and officers; and Hindu and Sikh leaders often found East India Company officials to be more overbearing than the familiar Muslim overlords.

The East India Company imposed its will chiefly through the army. Britons served as officers, but most of the soldiers were Indians, called sepoys. Often British officers scorned Indian religious beliefs and cultural practices. This disdain proved disastrous in 1857, when officers introduced the new Enfield rifle. When Indian soldiers learned that the new gun cartridges—which had to be bitten to release the gunpowder—had been greased with animal fat, they were enraged. Hindus and Muslims regarded the consumption animal fat to be vile and corrupting.

Thousands mutinied. This sparked a more general upheaval. In Delhi, the sepoys declared the last Mughal emperor—Bahadur Shah—to be their leader and urged others to rise up against the East India Company. Many Maratha princes also seized on this opportunity to challenge company rule. Rebel forces seized Delhi, Lucknow, and other cities in northern India, taking British soldiers and their families as captives. The East India Company eventually regrouped and, augmented by loyal Sikh soldiers, crushed the rebellion, which lasted nearly a year. As British and Sikh forces breached rebel defenses outside Delhi, the rebels massacred several hundred British women and children (Cawnpore Massacre). The British retaliation was equally brutal: sometimes rebel soldiers were strapped to cannon and blown to bits.

In the wake of the "Sepoy Mutiny," the British government dissolved the East India Company and decided to rule India directly as a colony of the crown. Queen Victoria would eventually become Empress of India, but real authority was wielded by the British prime minister, chosen by the majority in Parliament. A special cabinet post—Secretary for India—was charged with oversight of the colony. But the great distance to India required that most decisions be made in Calcutta by the governor general (now known as viceroy) of India. (During the sweltering summer months, many government functions were shifted to Simla [pronounced SHIM-lah], a military headquarters in the foothills of the Himalayas.) The powers of the viceroy were nearly absolute; his decisions were ultimately enforced by the army.

The viceroy directly ruled two-thirds of British India, which was initially divided into seven provinces: United Provinces, which encompassed much of the upper Ganges River plain; Bihar and Orissa, the lower Ganges; Bengal, the Ganges delta, including Calcutta; Madras, the long southern and eastern coast; Punjab, the high plateau, watered by five rivers, that stretched to Afghanistan; the Central Provinces, in the landlocked geographical center of the subcontinent; and Bombay, along the Arabian coast, including the city of Bombay (see Map A, p. 11). Provincial governors reported to the viceroy in Calcutta; and every province was further subdivided into districts—one for about every million inhabitants, each governed by a British administrator.

At each level, British officials were advised by a legislative council that usually included a handful of Indians. By the late 1800s the Royal Indian Army consisted of 200,000 soldiers. Of these, 60,000 soldiers, and all 2,000 of its officers, were British; another 140,000 soldiers were Indians. Whenever crises threatened public order—famine, cholera, riots—British officials would dispatch the Royal Indian Army to the scene of the trouble.

The actual administration of the colony was the work of the Indian Civil Service, which in 1880 consisted of about 1,000 senior members; all but a handful were British. Some worked for the viceroy in Calcutta and others with the provincial governors; still others worked at the district level. While the top officials in Calcutta and the provincial capitals were frequently rotated to different postings, the lesser officials established real power, by assessing and collecting taxes, keeping financial accounts, and processing the paperwork that is central to any modern bureaucracy.

But if the lines of British authority filled out vast organizational charts, British officials did not "rule" a land as vast and populous as India. Much like the Mughal officials before them, British administrators provided the overarching structure of government; but that structure was too thin—too poorly staffed and funded—to touch on the lives of most of the 250 million Indians who occupied a landmass the size of Europe (excluding Russia). Many villagers had never even seen a British official. For these Indians, responsible authority rested with local elites, such as religious leaders, *zamindars,* or village officials.

The British government's main task was to ensure the profitability of the colony—chiefly by preventing further uprisings. British officials promoted economic development and administrative efficiency by building railroads, bridges, and telegraph lines, and by embarking on irrigation and land reclamation projects. Officials also extolled the benefits of British civilization more generally, such as by establishing British-styled courts of law and founding universities and schools modelled after those in Great Britain.

British officials encouraged well-to-do Indians to educate their sons according to British models. A few attended universities in Calcuttta, Bombay, and Madras that had been based on the program at the University of London. British officials—along with missionaries and philanthropists—also established hundreds of primary and secondary schools based on British templates. Although instruction was usually provided in the regional languages of India—Bengali, Marathi, Punjabi, Gujarati—nearly all such schools included instruction in English. There were too few such schools to significantly improve literacy. According to the census of 1881, 95 percent of Indians could not read or write.

But viceroys rarely interfered with religious practices or the power of local elites. Occasionally an ambitious provincial governor or district administrator would seek to "reform" Indian life and culture—perhaps by prohibiting child marriage or by suppressing harsh treatment of widows and Untouchables. But interference in local economic or cultural practices carried the risk of alienating local religious and economic elites—and thus undermining the stability that was essential to efficient (and profitable) colonial administration.

PRINCELY INDIA

The third of India that did not fall under the direct jurisdiction of the British governor general consisted of some 600 "princely states" whose rulers were hereditary monarchs—mostly Hindu maharajas or Muslim nizams. Some of these states were enormous: Hyderabad, the land-locked principality in the south, had about 15 million people; Kashmir and Jammu, the remote mountain kingdom in the Himalayas, was nearly the size of Montana. Other princely states were tiny, consisting of only a few thousand inhabitants.

But virtually none of the Indian princes were independent; nearly all governed in "association" with the British government. When Great Britain took over rule from the East India Company, it also assumed responsibility for various treaties the company had negotiated with Indian princes and kings. As with the East India Company, a British "Resident" was assigned to advise and guide each prince; if the prince failed to keep order, incurred massive debts, or otherwise offended British sensibilities, the Resident could invoke legal powers or economic sanctions to undermine the prince or even drive him (or her) from power. When the elderly Nizam of Hyderabad fell ill, for example, relatives proposed that the Nizam's eight-year-old son and successor—Mir Osman Ali Khan—receive instruction from Muslim clerics and court officials. But the Resident rejected this educational scheme as excessively narrow.

Sometimes princes became dependent on British guidance and support; often they even became enamored of British customs and manners. Indian princes were usually educated by English tutors, attended schools in India built upon English models, or traveled to study in Britain. The ceremonial trappings of the British royalty—and of the English upper classes more generally—often resonated with the aspirations of Indian royalty. Indian rulers regularly mingled with English elites in London and took grand tours of Europe. To be sure, some princes chafed at British interference and arrogance; but the viceroys usually assumed, not without reason, that the princes would generally uphold the British Raj.

THE RISE OF INDIAN NATIONAL CONGRESS (INC)

Although Britain's modest educational initiatives failed to leave much of an imprint on the Indian masses, a significant number of high-caste Hindus had recognized that knowledge of English—and of British laws, customs, and preferences—would provide boundless opportunities for entrepreneurs, clerks, and civil servants. The natural pathway to such careers was to acquire a "British" education—and to learn English.

By the 1880s, an entire class of young "British-educated" men was advancing through the lower levels of the British military and civil services, or making gains in the new fields of law and medicine. But their ambitions were frustrated by the fact that Indians were mostly barred from top positions. Only a handful of the 1,000 top administrators in the British civil service were Indian, and none of the officers of the Royal Indian Army.

Young well-to-do Brahmans (high-caste Hindus), imbued with at least the rudiments of an English education and skilled in administration, had little hope of controlling the institutions they were themselves managing. They could supervise nearly all aspects of a district government—setting tax rates, collecting payments, and rendering accounts—but they could not actually make the final decisions on such matters. They could serve as key medical personnel, but not as directors of infirmaries and hospitals. They could work as clerks and legal assistants in the law courts, but only rarely as judges and prosecutors.

These young Indians inhabited two different worlds. By assimilating to the sensibilities and values of Britain, they were distancing themselves from the religious beliefs and cultural practices of their parents and grandparents. Their careers and lives were dependent on British institutions; but their aspirations were frustrated by those same institutions.

One such Indian was Surendranath Banerjea (1848–1926). His father, a Brahman and a doctor, wanted Surendranath to pursue a career in the Indian Civil Service. Because the examinations for such positions were held only in Britain, Banerjea traveled to London in 1868, but the registrar said he was too young to take the exam. The following year Banerjea passed the exam and was assigned to serve as magistrate in northern Bengal, one of the first Indians to hold such a position. But a subordinate made a clerical error which provided British supervisors with an excuse to dismiss Banerjea. Banerjea journeyed to London to appeal the decision, but his appeal was denied, as was his application to take the bar examinations. Embittered, Banerjea returned to Calcutta and committed his life to "redressing our wrongs and protecting our rights." In 1876 he founded the Indian Association, which became a significant forum for young British-educated Indians to air their frustration. Within a few years, British officials in Calcutta were complaining that public opinion in Bengal was "largely swayed by the views held by schoolboys."

In 1878 Viceroy Lord Lytton enacted several laws to prevent such resentments from erupting into rebellion. (The sepoy uprising was still fresh in the memory of every British administrator.) The Vernacular Press Act allowed British officials to suppress any newspapers published in Indian languages, while the Arms Act required Indians to register their guns with the government; Europeans were not required to do so. Indians seethed over these discriminatory measures.

Liberals in London, too, were unsettled by the blatant suppression of basic freedoms in India. Lord Ripon, who succeeded Lytton as governor general in 1880, sought to win over Indian leaders rather than crush them. He proposed to rescind the Vernacular Press Act and the Arms Act; and he also endorsed a law that allowed Indian judges to try cases involving European defendants. (At the time, Europeans accused of crimes could insist that their case be heard by a European judge.)

But Ripon's measures provoked a backlash from British officials in the Indian Civil Service—and from British businessmen in India. British tea and indigo planters resorted to racist caricature, conjuring images of Indian judges leering at British women in rape cases. Rudyard Kipling, the celebrated English writer who then lived in Lahore, reflected the resentments of British officialdom: "Race feeling has never been so high since the Mutiny." Ripon's reforms were defeated. The message to the Indian elite was clear: British officials and settlers would not relinquish power without a fight.

Indian leaders created regional organizations to press for political concessions. In 1885 they formed the All-Indian National Congress (INC). Its goal was not to overthrow British rule but to reform it. At its 1900 convention INC leader Achut Sitaran Sathe explained that the educated Indian regarded the English flag as his "physical shelter," and the English philosopher, his "spiritual consolation."

> The English renaissance has so far permeated the educated Indian that it is no longer possible for him to be otherwise than loyal and affectionate towards the rulers of his choice.

But if the early leaders of the INC did not preach sedition, most believed that they would ultimately rule India. Some cited the example of the Washington, Jefferson, and the American "Continental Congress" a century earlier. Others referenced the Italian nationalist, Mazzini, who had uprooted foreign overlords and unified Italy, or Irish nationalists, who were trying to push Britain out of Ireland. British-educated Indians had read John Stuart Mill, Herbert Spencer, and August Comte; they knew that in the not–too–distant future, Indian administrators, clerks, accountants, doctors, and engineers would run India themselves.

The British-educated leaders of the INC, however, were bedeviled by an insoluble conundrum. Although they claimed to speak for the impoverished and illiterate masses of India, the INC leaders themselves were often divorced from those masses. The INC focused on the discriminatory policies of the British civil service; but such issues mattered little to the peasant whose mud huts had been washed away in a storm; or to the villager who had fallen victim to the bubonic plague; or to the Untouchable who could not gain access to a water well or Hindu temple. For the leaders of the INC, the fact of their British education, of their assimilation to the values of modern England, ensured their political impotence among the Indian masses.

These British-educated Indians believed that they could somehow persuade Britain to transfer power to them; and once they ruled India, they would educate and uplift its struggling masses.

But this path to Indian nationhood was now challenged by a different type of leader with a different goal for India. These new leaders did not seek to uplift and modernize the impoverished masses of India, but instead resolved to champion the ideals of traditional India. They sought not to transform India into Britain, but to revitalize and enshrine Hindu values and ideals.

APOSTLES OF HINDU REVIVAL

Bankim Chandra Chatterji (1838–1894) was among the early proponents of Hindu revival. In 1858, as one of the two graduates of the first class of Calcutta University, Chatterji was hired as a deputy magistrate in the Indian Civil Service in Bengal. Denied the prospect of advancement— he remained in the same position for thirty-three years—Chatterji devoted himself to literary pursuits. Eschewing English models, he wrote in Bengali and Sanskrit and focused on Bengali people and culture. His 1882 novel, *Anandamath* ("Abbey of Bliss"), was set during the great famine of 1771, when Bengalis rose against the British. In the climactic scene, Indian rebels race across a bridge only to be cut down by artillery. Momentarily stunned, the rebels regroup, charge, and drive the British back. Throughout the action, Hindu monks and supernatural figures provide commentary. One godlike figure explains that there are two kinds of knowledge: physical and spiritual. While Hindus possess spiritual knowledge, the English brought knowledge of the physical world to Indians. Once they acquire that knowledge, Indians will reclaim their destiny by fusing spiritual and physical knowledge into a single, dynamic culture.

The central revelation of the novel featured a poem, the *Bandemataram* ("I praise thee, Mother"), which was put to music and was sung at the 1896 session of the Indian National Congress. In the poem, "Mother" referred both to Bengal and to the female component of the Hindu deity.

> Mother, I bow to thee!
> Rich with thy hurrying streams,
> Bright with thy orchard gleams,
> Cool with the winds of delight,
> Dark fields waving, Mother of might,
> Mother free.

The *Bandemataram* became the anthem of Indian nationalism.

Throughout Bengal, secret societies were formed to agitate for independence; but unlike the INC, which advocated political reform within the framework of British governance, proponents of Hindu revival saw Hinduism as both the means of achieving independence—and the chief goal of the movement. By building a strong Hindu nation, Hindus would secure its independence.

While Chatterji was inspiring Bengalis to reclaim Hindu values, Bal Gangadhar Tilak (1856–1920) was doing something similar among Marathi-speaking Hindus in Bombay, far to the west. Tilak, like Chatterji, had been among the first Indians to acquire a higher education in his region, receiving a bachelor's degree from Deccan College in 1877. Rather than enter the British civil service, Tilak founded the *Kesari,* a weekly newspaper written in Marathi and published in Bombay. If Chatterji evoked Bengali resistance to the British in 1711, Tilak celebrated the

Maratha warrior Shivaji. Tilak proposed two new annual festivals celebrating Hinduism—one dedicated to the Hindu god Ganesh, the other to Shiva.

During an outbreak of the bubonic plague in 1897, Tilak condemned British officials for intrusive searches and quarantines. He denounced by name Walter Charles Rand, the British officer in charge of the anti-plague measures, calling him "suspicious, sullen and tyrannical." Tilak's articles also cited the *Bhagavad Gita,* a sacred Hindu text, as justifications for insurrection. In the *Bhagavad Gita,* the deity Krishna (as the messenger, Arjuna) endorsed the killing even of teachers and kinsmen. Tilak noted that Shivaji, too, had waged bloody war against foreign oppressors. "Enter into the extremely high atmosphere of the *Bhagavad Gita,*" Tilak advised readers, "and then consider the actions of great men."

Several weeks later two teenaged Hindu brothers—Demodar and Balkrishna Chapekar—shot and killed Rand and his military attaché at Poona, near Bombay. The boys were charged with murder and Tilak, who had ties to militant Hindu secret societies, was charged with sedition and incitement to violence. The brothers were hanged; when the noose was placed around Demodar's neck, he was holding a copy of the *Bhagavad Gita.* Tilak was sentenced to eighteen months in prison. Sporadic strikes, boycotts, and riots broke out throughout the province.

Vinayak Savarkar (1883–1966), a Brahman, was sixteen when the Chapekar brothers were executed. He took a vow before the family deity, Durga, to complete the work of the Chapekars and drive the British from the motherland. He also resolved to follow the path of the great Hindu warrior, Shivaji. And like Tilak and other proponents of Hindu revival, Savarkar aspired to write serious literature in the vernacular. "Follow the laws of Nature," he wrote in Marathi in an early poem. "Little drops of water make the pond. Organize all Hindus and unify them." Savarkar founded a secret society in 1900, which spread through western and central India.

Then came the event that roused Hindus to action throughout Bengal.

THE PARTITION OF BENGAL AND HINDU TERRORISM

In 1899 Lord Curzon had assumed duties as the new viceroy of India. He resolved to reconcile Indians to British rule by treating them fairly. "The [Indian National] Congress is tottering to its fall," he declared in 1900.

Then in 1905 Curzon announced an ill-fated plan to divide Bengal into two provinces. On the surface, it made administrative sense. With 78 million people, Bengal was more populous than the entire United States. Bengali radicals, however, viewed the measure as a sinister ploy to fracture the increasingly militant epicenter of opposition to British rule—and to create a new province in east Bengal with a Muslim majority. Hindu revivalists perceived in Curzon's actions a manifestation of the British strategy of "divide and conquer": by dividing Bengal, the British rekindled tensions between Hindus and Muslims. The Indian National Congress also denounced the partition plan.

Hindu radicals insisted that words of protest were not enough. They first called for a boycott of all British-manufactured goods: this *swadeshi* movement sought to stem the flow of Indian wealth to Britain. In Poona, Savarkar—after meeting with Tilak—proposed to collect heaping piles of British goods and burn them in public squares. These bonfires, illegal and provocative, unsettled the INC. Mohandas Gandhi, a legal advocate for the rights of Indians in South Africa, observed that a people could never achieve true liberation through acts of violence. Savarkar replied that liberation would occur no other way.

By 1907 the Indian National Congress was being pulled in two directions: one, secular and British in orientation, sought to attain independence through constitutional reform; the other, led by Tilak, Savarkar, and the revivalists, was Hindu and extremist; it insisted that Indians would seize control of the nation only by force. Tilak proposed to extend the boycott, which had focused on Bengal and the region around Poona, to all of India. The next year, two Bengalis, intent on assassinating a harsh British judge, threw a bomb that killed two British women. One of the youths committed suicide; the other was hanged. Talik wrote searing editorials in defense of the militants; he was convicted of sedition and sentenced to six years in prison in Burma.

In 1909 a group of Hindu militants who took inspiration, and probably guidance, from Savarkar, shot and killed a British tax collector and threw a bomb at Viceroy Lord Minto. Savarkar fled from London to Paris, where he was apprehended. He was shipped to India where he was convicted of terrorism and sedition and was sentenced to fifty years in prison. He was then sent to prison in the Andaman Islands.

THE MUSLIM LEAGUE

The furor over the partition of Bengal did not just fracture the INC; it unnerved the Muslim leaders of India. For decades, India's better-educated Muslims had followed the precepts of Syed Ahmad Khan (1817–1898), a Muslim scholar who spent much of his life trying to reconcile Muslim beliefs with science and reason. Khan had disagreed with Muslim clerics who clung to what he regarded as "medieval" superstitions. He insisted that the *Qur'an,* understood properly, was fully compatible with modern science. Khan urged Indians, and especially Muslim leaders, to endorse and uphold British rule. If the British were driven from India, he warned, the overwhelming Hindu majority would impose their "medieval" religion and culture upon Muslims.

By 1906, Khan's warnings resonated with force. That year wealthy Muslims responded to Hindu political activism by forming the All-India Muslim League (hereafter, the Muslim League). Its purpose was to defend Muslim interests and promote "feelings of loyalty to the British government." Muslims, a vulnerable minority, should buttress the British Raj rather than pull it down.

British officials, appreciative of Muslim support, responded favorably to the Muslim League. They agreed to "protect" Muslims by designating some seats in legislative councils as "reserved" for Muslims. This special treatment infuriated the INC: the British made no similar provision for protecting the Hindu minority in Bengal. Tensions smoldered.

WORLD WAR I

In 1914 all of Europe was plunged into the Great War. Within a few months Britain was mired in brutal trench warfare against Germany and the rest of the Central Powers. Some Indians saw this as the moment to drive the British from India. One was M. N. Roy (1887–1954), a founder of the Communist Party of India. Born a Brahman in a village near Calcutta, Roy was drawn as a teenager to Savarkar's militant Hindu societies. Roy was arrested during anti-British protests—and swiftly released because of his age. He then shifted from Hindu extremism to communist revolution. Again he was arrested, this time during a robbery to fund the revolution; he was later released. When Britain went to war with Germany, Roy conspired with German agents to smuggle guns to Indian revolutionaries in Bengal.

British officials caught wind of the scheme and moved to arrest Roy, who fled to the United States and enrolled as a student at Stanford. But he continued to meet with German diplomats. In 1917, after the United States entered the war, Roy was arrested. While out on bail, he fled to Mexico and joined radicals in the new Mexican republic. Soon he became embroiled in a theoretical dispute with Lenin and, later, with Stalin. (Roy sought to build grassroots revolutionary cells among colonial peoples like the Indians; Lenin and Stalin sought to support "bourgeois" independence movements, such as the INC, in order to swiftly weaken major imperialist powers, such as Britain and Germany.)

Many Indian leaders, however, supported Britain during the Great War. From prison Savarkar wrote that he was delighted that Indians were volunteering to fight for Britain in Europe: "Manliness after all is not dead yet in the land." Most INC leaders also endorsed the British war effort. They reasoned that if they helped Great Britain in its hour of need, a grateful British government would reciprocate by transferring power to the INC after the war.

During the Great War, nearly a million Indians fought for Great Britain, many seeing action in the Middle East, North Africa, and France.

ENTER GANDHI, AZAD, AND JINNAH

During these years there arrived one of the pivotal figures in the history of India, and of the twentieth century. Mohandas Gandhi (1868–1948) was an unexceptional youth. He was born into a merchant caste in Gujarat (western India). His parents sent him to local English-style schools—he ranked in the middle of his class—and they arranged for his marriage when he was thirteen. When his father died, relatives recommended that young Gandhi be sent to study law in London as preparation for the Indian Civil Service.

Gandhi left India—as well his wife and young son. When he arrived in London, he sought to assimilate into British culture and values. He studied French and took dancing and violin lessons; wore a high silk hat, spats, and patent leather boots, and even carried a silver-mounted walking stick. But he could not abide—or even digest—English food. He ate meals with vegetarians and increasingly socialized with scholars of Indian culture. Though his mother had been a devout Hindu, Gandhi now rediscovered the *Bhagavad Gita* and other Hindu texts. As he was drawn to a deeper engagement with classic Indian texts, he viewed English society and culture with growing skepticism.

In 1891 he passed the bar exam and returned to India. But no administrative job was forthcoming and he lacked the contacts and the knowledge of Indian legal procedures to set up his own law practice. Eventually he found work with Indian businessmen in South Africa. Gandhi's job was to help defend the Indians' interests against the racist apartheid regime. From 1893 to 1914, Gandhi emerged as a formidable political organizer and champion of Indian rights in South Africa.

During these years, moreover, Gandhi experienced a profound spiritual transformation. He rejected the trappings of British culture along with much of its substance. He denounced the hulking steel mills of Manchester, the oppressive character of industrial work, the hopeless amorality of the big cities. Modernity, he said, leached human beings of their souls. Increasingly he embraced the life of the simple Indian peasant. He went barefoot and wore traditional Indian clothing made of homespun, handwoven cloth (*khadi*).

Gandhi also rejected violence as an instrument for social change. He urged oppressed peoples to pursue justice through nonviolent civil disobedience, a policy he called *satyagraha*—"truth force." The **way** that people attained justice, he insisted, inevitably permeated the results that ensued. Those who resorted to violence against unjust rule were themselves corrupted by that violence; conversely, those who were animated by love and truth ultimately prevailed against those imbued with hatred and evil.

On his return to India in 1915, however, Gandhi endorsed the British government's war effort. He insisted that fighting for Britain and France was tantamount to fighting for India's independence.

Though mostly unknown in India, Gandhi sought to heal divisions between India's Hindus and Muslims. A key ally was Abul Kalam Azad (1888–1958), whose wealthy father had raised the boy to become a Muslim scholar. But as a young man he soon went his own way; he chose as his pen name—Azad—which means free, to signify his growing intellectual independence. Increasingly he insisted that Islam manifested the fundamental truths of all religions, which resonated with a similar belief among Hindu scholars concerning the universality of **their** religion. Azad urged Muslims and Hindus to work together to secure India's independence.

Mohammad Ali Jinnah (1876–1948), the son of a Muslim businessman in Karachi, also assumed the political compatibility of Hindus and Muslims: government could avoid communal divisions by insisting on a secular orientation. Jinnah had served as an apprentice in a trading company in London as a young man. He left the apprenticeship to study the law, receiving a degree in 1895. He returned to Bombay the next year, where he became a wealthy lawyer. Jinnah joined the Indian National Congress and was elected to serve in the Bombay legislature; he also joined the Muslim League and became one of its leaders.

In 1916, at a pivotal meeting at Lucknow, Jinnah persuaded Motilal Nehru (1861–1931), a British-educated lawyer who had been president of the INC, and other INC leaders to accept a framework for a future constitution of India, where much of the governing power would rest with the governments of each province. The leaders agreed to significant compromise:

> 1) In provinces where Hindus outnumbered Muslims (Bombay, United Province, Bihar), specific seats in the legislature would be reserved for Muslims **in excess** of their percentage within the overall population of that province: that would help protect the Muslim minority;

> 2) In provinces where Muslims outnumbered Hindus (Bengal and the Punjab), the number of seats reserved for Muslims would be **reduced.** This would prevent the Muslims from controlling the provincial government and thus help protect the Hindu minority in those provinces.

The Lucknow Pact, by joining Muslim and Hindu leaders, strengthened the nationalist campaign: if the peoples of India were united, colonial control could not long endure.

Britain responded to this initiative, and to the grinding losses of a seemingly interminable war in Europe, by ceding more power to Indians at the provincial level. There Britain endorsed the principle of "dyarchy": each British provincial governor would share power with ministers chosen by (mostly) elected Indian legislatures. (The principle of dyarchy did not extend to matters of finance, police, and the courts.) Many Indians regarded these reforms as first steps toward the postwar goal of independence.

THE ROWLATT ACTS, THE AMRITSAR MASSACRE, AND "NONCOOPERATION"

On November 11, 1918 an armistice was signed ending the Great War. But instead of granting independence, as most Indian leaders had assumed, Britain extended wartime emergency restrictions into the peace. These repressive laws, known as the Rowlatt Acts, gave Britain the power to arrest "terrorist" suspects, imprison them immediately, and try them without juries.

Leaders of the INC felt betrayed. The Rowlatt acts, Gandhi declared, were "a striking demonstration of the determination of the Civil Service to retain its grip of our necks." Gandhi then issued a threat: "I can no longer render peaceful obedience to the laws of a power that is capable of such a piece of devilish legislation." He urged Indians to join him on a *satyagraha* campaign against the acts. He called for a general strike—Indians should not report for work or school; they should instead pray or fast, or attend political meetings. Muslims, Hindus, Sikhs and other Indians joined in these protests.

But in Amritsar, the largest city in the Punjab, the protests turned violent and four Europeans were killed. Britain imposed martial law. When a group of unarmed civilians peacefully gathered in the Jallianwalla Bagh, a walled-in public square, British troops opened fire, killing 400 and wounding many more. Protests and riots erupted throughout the Punjab. Gandhi cancelled the remainder of the *satyagraha,* saying that he had been guilty of a "Himalayan miscalculation" by encouraging Indians to disobey the law before they had fully absorbed the lessons of nonviolence.

Though his campaign had failed, Gandhi had become the most visible Indian on the subcontinent. Soon he was leader of the INC; some began referring to him as the *mahatma*—great soul. British officials were unnerved by this new challenge to imperial rule. "Gandhi is incapable of hurting a fly and is as honest as the day," the viceroy confided to his superiors in London, "but he enters quite lightheartedly on a course of action that may lead to much hardship to people who are ignorant and easily led astray."

After months of prayer and reflection, Gandhi insisted that India could win independence without violent insurrection. He proposed a new campaign of "noncooperation": Indians should boycott foreign goods, withdraw children from schools, and refuse to take part in the legislative elections. He also encouraged Indians to spin their own cloth—as he did himself. "Love of foreign cloth," Gandhi declared, "brought foreign domination, pauperism and what is worse, shame to many a home." The simple white hat, made of homespun cloth (*khadi*)—the "Gandhi cap"—became the symbol of the nationalist cause.

To be sure, some INC leaders were unpersuaded by this strategy. Those who had been elected to the provincial legislatures and had taken office within the "dyarchy" system were reluctant to surrender power.

But in 1921 Gandhi went ahead with the "noncooperation" crusade. He traveled throughout India, walking dozens of miles a day to visit remote villages. His challenge to British rule exacerbated tensions; riots erupted in Bombay and elsewhere. INC leaders nevertheless sought to intensify the campaign. In 1922 Gandhi complied by endorsing nonviolent civil disobedience: it was not enough to refuse to cooperate with British rule—Indians should challenge injustice by breaking unjust laws. Specifically, Indians should not pay taxes that funded British rule.

A few days later, February 4, 1922, rioters in the town of Chauri Chaura in the United Provinces surrounded the police station and set it ablaze, killing twenty-two. Gandhi was devastated. "God spoke clearly through Chauri Chaura," he declared. "He has warned me that there is not yet in India that nonviolent and truthful atmosphere which alone can justify mass civil disobedience." He called off the civil disobedience campaign. By then, Britain had already ordered his arrest on charges of sedition. He spent the next two years in prison.

Gandhi had nevertheless mobilized the diverse elements of Indian nationalism. Perhaps his most surprising achievement had been to win over the younger generation of mostly secular, British-educated Indian leaders. Jawaharlal Nehru (1889–1964) was the most important of these. The son of Motilal Nehru, Jawaharlal grew up in a wealthy family in Delhi, attended Cambridge University, and was admitted to the London bar in 1912. Soon afterward he returned to India. But while Gandhi repudiated British culture and modernity, young Nehru was drawn to Marxism. He believed that while British industrialists and financiers exploited the Indian peoples, so did the Indian *zamindars*. Nehru endorsed communist revolution in principle, and applauded the Bolshevik takeover of Russia in 1917. But he was more lawyer than bomb-throwing revolutionary. And so he gravitated to Gandhi, partly because of the Mahatma's compelling personality, but also because Nehru believed that Gandhi, uniquely attuned to the Hindu masses, could enlist their support to expel the British from India. Afterward, Indians could be taught the principles of Marxist socialism. Or so Nehru imagined.

Confirmed communists, less fearful of violence, exploited the chaos for their own purposes following Gandhi's campaign. Some revolutionaries led peasant uprisings and rent strikes in Bengal, Bihar, and Hyderabad; others organized industrial workers in Bombay, Calcutta, and Delhi. In 1928 Lajpat Rai, known as "the lion of the Punjab," led a protest that culminated in a police charge; Rai was himself struck. He managed to deliver a rousing speech—"The blows struck against me will be the last nails in the coffin of British rule in India"—but he died several weeks later. Enraged, twenty-three-year-old Bhagat Singh, a Sikh revolutionary with ties to several communist cells, threw a bomb at the police offer who had ordered the attack on Rai. The bomb missed the officer but killed two young British women. Singh was hanged—and immediately became a martyr to the cause. The following year Indian communists organized a successful strike of railway workers; dozens of communist leaders were imprisoned.

Perhaps the most important legacy of Gandhi's civil disobedience campaign was the resurgence of Hindu radicalism. Once mobilized for political action, many Hindus joined the Hindu Mahasabha, which spearheaded a campaign to promote Hindu values and practices, including cow protection. Savarkar, released from prison in 1924, became its leader. His *Hindutva: Who is a Hindu* (1923), which had been smuggled out of prison and published, insisted that all the peoples of the Indian subcontinent—whether Sikh, Muslim, or Hindu—shared the common core values of Hindu civilization. Savarkar's broad claims reinforced the cultural themes of Hindu revivalists—India's destiny was to become a great Hindu nation: Hindustan.

IQBAL AND THE MUSLIM RESURGENCE

Many Muslims were alarmed by these developments. Those who had endorsed Islamic revival and "self-strengthening" campaigns redoubled their efforts. Those who had believed that constitutional structures could protect the Muslim minority now had doubts. Muslims had good reason to worry about their fate in a government dominated by Savarkar and the Hindu Mahasabha.

A key figure in the Islamic revival was Muhammad Iqbal (1873–1938). Born in Sialkot in the Punjab, Iqbal attended the local *madrasah* (Islamic school) and local British-style colleges, and then was sent to the Government College at Lahore, where he graduated in 1899. He studied English literature and Persian at Cambridge, was admitted to the London bar, and earned a PhD at a German university, completing a dissertation on Persian philosophy. In 1908 he returned to Lahore to teach at the Government College.

Iqbal became an international literary figure. He wrote mostly poetry, usually in Urdu or Persian, which he regarded as a way of addressing the problems confronting the Muslims of India. "The psychologist swims," he wrote in 1910. "The poet dives." Iqbal emphasized the importance of the Muslim community—"the single bond" that grew out of a shared faith. By contrast, Indian politics had become a welter of "dismembered tribes," each at odds with the other. Any attempt to stitch these remnants into a single nation would fail.

In 1930 Iqbal, then president of the Muslim League, declared that the peoples of India were largely defined by their religious communities—and each religious community required its own nation-state. "The construction of a polity on national lines, if it means a displacement of Islamic principles of solidarity, is simply unthinkable to a Muslim," he explained. Muslims deserved their own state, though it was not yet clear whether this referred to a largely autonomous province within an Indian federation or to a completely separate nation-state.

GANDHI AND THE SALT MARCH: 1930–1932

During the 1930s "communal riots"—those between the Muslim and Hindu communities—erupted frequently. Communist revolutionaries incited peasants and industrial workers. Then the Great Depression struck. Famines and epidemics made matters even worse. Britain's hold on the colony appeared to be slipping.

Gandhi now mounted a new civil disobedience campaign. He decided to challenge the British monopoly on salt, an essential commodity in such a warm climate. After announcing his plans, he commenced a 240-mile *satyagraha* walk from Ahmedabad to the salt flats on the Arabian coast at Dandi. He was joined by several dozen supporters, most of whom carried copies of the *Bhagavad Gita*. Jawaharlal Nehru, one of the marchers, would never forget the sight of the elderly Mahatma:

> I saw him marching staff in hand . . . Here was a pilgrim on his quest of Truth, quiet, peaceful, determined and fearless, who would continue that quest and pilgrimage regardless of consequences.

Four weeks later Gandhi arrived at Dandi, with thousands marching behind. He scooped up a handful of mud and salt and gave it away—in defiance of the British monopoly on salt production. The protests at Dandi intensified, triggering riots and confrontations throughout India. Eventually Gandhi was arrested, along with some 50,000 supporters.

The "salt march" succeeded in drawing millions of Indians into political action; but it failed to bring an end to British rule—or even to cancellation of the salt tax. It also raised questions about the efficacy of civil disobedience. M. N. Roy, the communist revolutionary who had recently sneaked back into India, attacked Gandhian nonviolence as a "subtle intellectual device for concealing the capitalist exploitation of the country." At the other political extreme, the Hindu radical Savarkar also repudiated Gandhi's strategy: "We denounce the doctrine of absolute non-violence not because we are less saintly, but because we are more sensible." Even mainstream leaders of the INC, many of whom ended up in prison, were perplexed. Gandhi had indeed managed to "shake the foundations of the British Empire." But the empire still stood.

THE "PROBLEM" OF THE UNTOUCHABLES

Another question complicated matters further: what was to be done about India's 70 million Untouchables? Defending their interests had been the lifework of Bhimrao Ramji (1891–1956), whose father had served in the British military. Himself an Untouchable, Ramji had nevertheless saved enough money to send Bimrao to school. As an Untouchable, however, Bimrao could not sit at desks with the other students but instead was obliged to sit on the floor at the side of the room. Other boys refused to come near him, or allow him to join in cricket or other games. His teachers would not touch his notebook, lest they become "polluted" from contact with him. One kind teacher, however, offered him special instruction—and food. The teacher's name was Ambedkar, which a grateful Bhimrao added to his own name. B. R. Ambedkar soon excelled in school and caught the attention of a local prince, who arranged for the boy to attend a local college and, later, Columbia University in New York. Ambedkar eventually received a PhD in economics from Columbia. His dissertation analyzed the economic problems of the Untouchables.

In 1918 Ambedkar returned to India to work on behalf of Untouchables. By the late 1920s he was leading *satyagraha* campaigns to gain Untouchables access to water wells and Hindu temples. But he insisted that the root cause of their problems lay in their powerlessness. He reasoned that the British had resolved to protect the Muslim minority by "reserving" seats for them in the provincial legislatures, and the British should do the same for Untouchables.

In 1932, when Gandhi was still in prison for his salt protest, the viceroy agreed to "reserve" seventy-one seats in the various provincial legislatures for Untouchables. As Ambedkar had insisted, moreover, Untouchables would vote as a "separate" electorate: every polling station would include a special ballot box only to be used by Untouchables. This would prevent well-to-do Hindus from electing "their" Untouchables, who could be expected to vote as their employers dictated.

Now Gandhi stormed into this debate. He had long deplored the treatment of Untouchables, whom he called *Harijans* (children of god), and he had worked tirelessly to improve their lives. But he was outraged by the British decision to grant Untouchables reserved seats and their own "separate" electorate. Untouchables should not be set apart from Indian society, but integrated within it more effectively. Gandhi also insisted that Untouchables had once been part of an indissoluble social order in the traditional villages of India, where people of all castes and religions lived in harmony. He argued that Britain had undermined this unity so as to ensure the subjugation Indian people. British acceptance of Ambedkar's plan was another manifestation of their longstanding policy of "divide and rule."

Gandhi announced that he would "fast unto death" if Britain did not withdraw its plan to reserve seats in the legislatures for Untouchables, chosen from their "separate" electorate. Then he stopped eating.

Ambedkar was now subjected to a firestorm of opposition. INC editors denounced him as a potential murderer. In the end Ambedkar had little choice but to withdraw his demand for a separate electorate for Untouchables. He reluctantly accepted reserved seats for Untouchables, a proposal the British accepted. INC leaders who regarded the rights of Untouchables as a distraction from the larger goal of assuming political power, now encouraged Gandhi to step down as their leader.

Meanwhile Ambedkar, furious, pondered whether he should encourage Untouchables to convert to Buddhism, Islam, or other religions.

GOVERNMENT OF INDIA ACT OF 1935

Although Gandhi's salt march failed to bring about the collapse of the British Empire, it forced Britain to initiate further reforms. These were institutionalized in the Government of India Act (1935). While retaining the British viceroy as the ultimate source of authority for all of India, the act provided for the election of provincial legislators, who would choose the top provincial ministers. In addition, more Indians, including women, gained the right to vote. Finally, some seats within the provincial legislatures were "reserved" for vulnerable minorities. The legislature of Bombay, for example, consisted of 175 seats. Of these, 15 were reserved for Untouchables, 29 for Muslims, and 17 for Christians, tribal peoples, and others. The remaining 114 seats were for the general population—that is, Hindus.

The British insisted that this constitution simultaneously recognized the democratic aspirations of the Indian people while protecting the rights of vulnerable minorities.[1] Most leaders of the INC were unhappy with the proposal: they criticized Britain for viewing India as an agglomeration of peoples rather than as a unified nation. But other nationalists realized that in most provinces—such as Bombay—the INC would dominate the legislature and thereby acquire real power. In the end, the INC criticized the 1935 Act but ran candidates for the provincial legislatures. And, as expected, the INC won legislative majorities in seven provinces.

These results confirmed the fears of the Muslim League, which fared poorly even in those provinces with a Muslim majority. Worse news came in 1937, when INC ministers took power in those seven provinces. Some INC-dominated provincial governments promoted Hindu symbols and culture, such as by flying the flag of the INC, singing the *Bandemataram,* endorsing the Hindu Mahasabha, and implementing Gandhi's vocational education scheme.

Such disputes persuaded Jinnah and other leaders of the Muslim League that Iqbal had been right: the only way to safeguard the Muslims of India was to provide for them their own state. In March 1940 the Muslim League endorsed Jinnah's resolution calling for the transformation of

---

1. The Government of India Act had also called for combining the British provinces with the princely states to form a single Indian federation, allowing for considerable provincial autonomy. But the princely states rejected this proposal.

the Muslim-majority provinces of northwest India and Bengal into autonomous states that could be grouped into one or more larger sovereign states. Europeans and Americans might be able to compartmentalize their lives into religious and secular components, but religion was an all-consuming aspect of the lives of India's Muslims. They must have their own state, with their own government.

WORLD WAR II AND THE "QUIT INDIA" MOVEMENT

By the spring of 1940, however, British prime minister Winston Churchill had more pressing concerns. Britain was at war with Hitler's Germany; the British viceroy of India also declared war—without conferring with Indian ministers. The INC initially offered to support the British war effort, in return for an immediate transfer of power to a central Indian government with a promise of complete independence after the war. The viceroy declared that Britain could not transfer power during the war; nor could the British government ignore its responsibilities to protect the Muslim, Sikh, and other minorities. There would be no deal with the INC.

The INC leaders who controlled the provincial governments resigned. Gandhi, Nehru, and other leaders vowed to resist the British war effort.

In December 1941, Japan attacked the American fleet at Pearl Harbor and then attempted to overrun British positions in East Asia. In March 1942, Japan seized Singapore and then moved on Southeast Asia and India. Churchill now dispatched Sir Stafford Cripps to enlist the support of Indian leaders by offering a new postwar constitution for India. The Cripps proposal would establish, after the war, an Indian union within the British Commonwealth. Any Indian province (or princely state) would have the right to remain outside of the Indian union and could join the Commonwealth as an independent state. In return for this future constitution, Cripps asked Indian leaders to promise to provide "the military, moral and material resources of India" in support of the war.

The INC rejected the Cripps offer. They recalled that Britain had reneged on its promises during the First World War. Equally important, the Cripps proposal obliged the INC to accept the possibility that the Muslim majority provinces and the princely states could secede from some future "Indian union."

The failure of the Cripps proposal did not dismay Churchill. One of his advisers noted that Churchill had literally danced for joy on hearing the news: he wanted to retain India as a British colony.

But doubtless he sat down swiftly on learning that Gandhi, now seventy-three, had vowed to intensify his campaign against British rule. Gandhi proposed a new civil disobedience campaign against Great Britain—even as Japanese armies were slashing through Burma and threatening India. Within India, tensions mounted. Should Indians remain in the British army or the Indian Civil Service? Should Hindu nationalists support the Japanese invaders? Should Muslims take over their own majoritarian provinces?

Gandhi was unrepentant: "I have made up my mind that it would be a good thing if a million people were shot in a brave and nonviolent rebellion against the British rule." When his friends, most of them apostles of nonviolence, dismissed his words as hyperbole, Gandhi retorted: "They do not know the fire that is raging in my breast."

On August 8, 1942, with Gandhi back as its leader, the INC passed the "Quit India" resolution, which demanded the immediate withdrawal of Britain. "We shall either free India or die in the attempt; we shall not live to see the perpetuation of our slavery."

Several hours later, the British arrested and imprisoned Gandhi along with all of the leaders of the INC. Britain also shut down INC newspapers and outlawed the organization.

What followed was the worst challenge to British rule since the Sepoy Mutiny nearly a century earlier. Students rioted in the major cities, overturning buses and cars. Protesters attacked hundreds of railway stations, post offices, and government officers. Telegraph lines were pulled down and railway bridges and tracks were blown up. In many parts of India, government operations evaporated. Anarchy beckoned. Britain imposed martial law.

Not all Indians, however, supported the "Quit India" movement:

> 1) The Communist Party, taking orders from Stalin, joined the British war effort: by 1942, Hitler's war machine had gobbled up much of the Soviet Union. Britain was now allied with Stalin's Soviet Union. Stalin ordered India's communists to fight for Britain— and therefore against the fascists of Hitler;

> 2) Jinnah and the Muslim League agreed to support the British war effort in return for British promises to include the League in any postwar independence solution; some Muslims took positions in the provincial governments left vacant by INC resignations;

> 3) Ambedkar, leader of the Untouchables, saw the retreat of the INC as a chance to push Untouchables into positions of power; he himself accepted a position on the Executive Council of the British Governor General;

> 4) Many of the rulers of the princely states supported Great Britain in order to cement their positions after the war: for example, in 1941, the nizam of Hyderabad provided funding for two squadrons of Royal Airforce fighter bombers; and Hari Singh, the maharaja of Kashmir, was named to Churchill's Imperial War Cabinet.

The war years were difficult. The leaders of the INC languished in jail. Tensions between Muslims and Hindus smoldered. A severe famine, exacerbated by the British diversion of grain, took the lives of several million Bengalis.

The Japanese invasion of India was stopped at the border. Britain, supported by the United States, held off the Japanese army, and then drove it back. In 1945 Germany surrendered and Japan was on the verge of collapse.

Now, at last, the postwar fate of India loomed ever larger.

Would Britain, at long last, grant independence? Would it propose a federated union of British provinces and princely states? Would it allow the Muslim-majority provinces to form their own Muslim states, or even combine to form "Pakistan"? Would it make provision to protect vulnerable minorities such as the Untouchables and the Sikhs? Would it, in light of the likelihood of violence, retain India as a colony of the British crown?

Schedule of Assignments and Class Activities

The schedule that follows assumes a class of about twenty students. Larger classes may require more time to allow all roles to be voiced and debated. If more than twelve class sessions are scheduled, the extra time can be used to develop more thoroughly the history of India and the ideas outlined in Appendices A–C. Students should begin readings in advance of class.

Schedule OF ASSIGNMENTS AND CLASS ACTIVITIES		
Class	**Class Activity**	**Student Activity before and during Class**
1	Introduction to Hinduism and Islam	Read "The Train to Simla, June 1945" and be prepared to discuss Appendix A: Hinduism and the *Bhagavad Gita* and Appendix B: Muhammad and the *Qur'an*; also read *Bhagavad Gita*, Books 1–4, 11, available online. Discuss in class.
2	Discussion of historical context; Assign role(s) to Governor(s) General	Read and be prepared to discuss "Unfinished Journey: From the Mughals to the British Raj and Beyond"
3	Discussion of Indian thinkers from Appendix C (Major Documents); Assign remainder of roles; Meet with Governor(s) General	Read Appendix C: Major Documents. In class: final 15 minutes: role distribution
4	Meet with factions, individual players	Read materials pertaining to your role; prepare for quiz on readings; meet with factions
5	Quiz in factions / Welcome by Governor(s) General	Quiz administered to factions / individual leaders. Final 10 minutes: official welcome from Governors General
6	Game: Full session 1	Sikhs, Nizam (Hyderabad), Maharaja (Kashmir), Communists: presentations to full session (prepare and submit paper #1)
7	Game: Full session 2	Dr. Ambedkar, Hindu Mahasabha, Gandhi adherents presentations (paper #1)
8	Game: Full session 3	INC, Muslim League: presentations to full session (paper #1)
9	Game: Full session 4	Governor(s) General issue draft recommendations, followed by open discussion
10	Game: Full session 5	Reply by various parties (second papers)
11	Game: Full session 6	Reply, continued / implementation of revised plan (Governors General option) (second papers)
12	Postmortem discussion: Game issues, Historical outcome; Hand out game evaluations	First 10 minutes: New government / Prime Minister gives speech outlining plans for future

Special Rules: Departures from the Historical Context

The game seeks to replicate the situation at Simla in June 1945, but it offers several counterfactual premises.

OMISSION OF LORD WAVELL

The game hypothesizes that Lord Wavell died, suddenly and of natural causes, just days after making his radio address of June 14, 1945. He has been replaced by one (or perhaps more) British Interim Governor(s) General. They will not only direct the proceedings of the conference, they will also supervise whatever functions are still held by the British government in India. They can make decisions as they see fit, subject to review by their superiors in the Foreign Office in London, and by the Prime Minister (i.e., the Gamemaster). The Prime Minister may promote the Governors General to Viceroy(s) if he is pleased with their performance.

INCLUSION OF THE NIZAM OF HYDERABAD AND THE MAHARAJA OF KASHMIR

Since 1857, Great Britain ruled much of India directly. But when Britain consolidated its hold on the subcontinent in the nineteenth century, it sometimes eschewed direct rule and instead entered into treaty relationships with hundreds of native Indian princes, who held titles such as "nawab" and "Nizam." These treaties generally allowed princes to retain sovereignty over their lands and subjects, and placed the princes under the protection of the British military, but ceded to the British government vast powers pertaining to foreign affairs and military matters. Thus the fate of the subcontinent is now complicated by the existence of these "dependent" native princes.

If, for example, Britain withdraws from India and gives the keys to its governmental buildings and operations to Gandhi and the Indian National Congress, the largest of the Indian nationalist organizations, the effect on the hundreds of "dependent" principalities would be unclear. Thus the withdrawal of Britain from the Indian subcontinent would oblige each of the princes to work out his own arrangements with whatever authority replaced Britain elsewhere on the subcontinent. There remains, too, the question of whether Britain can legally withdraw from these treaties unilaterally.

In fact, the British did **not** invite the Indian princes to the Simla conference, and instead called them to a separate meeting of the "Princely States," proceedings that were scrutinized by Indian nationalists. However, the game assumes that the two sets of meetings—that with the most prominent leaders of Indian nationalism and that with the independent princes—were joined into a single meeting at Simla.

The most important of these princes, and the one who will serve as a surrogate representing, loosely, most of the other Muslim princes, is the Nizam of Hyderabad (Nee-ZAAHM of HIGH-der-ih-bad); large classes might also include Hari Singh, the Hindu Maharaja of Kashmir.

INCLUSION OF THE HINDU MAHASABHA

The British Governors General also did not invite adherents of the Hindu Mahasabha (mah-hah-sah-ba). The Hindu Mahasabha was a Hindu cultural organization, not a political group. However, its ardent championing of the Hindu cause (protection of cows and Hindu shrines, advancement of Hindi as the language of the government, instruction in the classic texts of Hinduism) had political implications. Some members of the Hindu Mahasabha have created a paramilitary political arm known as the RSS. By mobilizing Hindu sentiment and channeling it at times into militant opposition, these Hindu radicals perhaps possess the power to wreck any decisions brokered at Simla. Thus, while the leaders of the Hindu Mahasabha did not attend the conference, their views—potentially shared by 300 million Hindus—loomed over its proceedings. The game mirrors that virtual presence by including an actual leader of the Mahasabha at the conference.

INCLUSION OF THE COMMUNIST PARTY LEADERSHIP

Some games also include a leader of the Communist Party of India, although the British did not invite the Communist leadership to Simla or to any other organizational meeting. Prime Minister Churchill is profoundly suspicious of Soviet Premier Stalin, and he has insisted that British officials closely monitor the Communist Party in India. In 1928 a series of labor disturbances swept through the major industrial cities, especially Bombay. The next year, the British arrested some thirty Communist leaders for conspiracy to overthrow British rule, and they were convicted and sent to prison. In the 1930s the Congress included in its list of complaints against the British the conviction of these Communists. Although the Soviet Union was allied to Great Britain during World War II, the British leaders in India will doubtless keep a close watch on the Communist Party.

INCLUSION OF INDETERMINATES

Nearly all versions of this game will include indeterminates. Some roles, moreover, contain substantial latitude in many matters. Thus, while it may seem that everyone at Simla has his own preset positions, this is wrong. The Governors General are new to India, and thus they will likely be responsive to what they hear and learn at Simla. Even the major parties—such as Congress and the Muslim League—contain a range of viewpoints. In larger classes, one member within each of these groups is undecided about many issues concerning the goals and strategies of the organizations to which he or she belongs. This person's decision will define those goals and strategies. Some roles will be defined as indeterminate: a "representative" or "spokesperson" for "rural India," or a "representative" or "spokesperson" for "urban India." Although no such person was convened at Simla, these players in some way represent undecided public opinion. They will thus have considerable influence in the event of referenda or elections.

DURATION OF THE SIMLA CONFERENCE

Historically, the Wavell-Simla conference lasted only a month: June 1945. It immediately became mired in a series of sharp disputes between leaders of Congress and the Muslim League. A particularly acrimonious issue was that of Muslim representation in a post-independence legislature. Congress included among its delegation Maulana Azad [sometimes identified as Maulana Abdul Kalam Azad], a prominent Muslim politician. Mohammed Ali Jinnah, leader of the Muslim League, insisted that it alone represented the Muslims of India and demanded that Congress drop Azad from its delegation. Congress, led by Jawaharlal Nehru and others, refused. This impasse wrecked the conference.

For the purposes of the game, the Simla conference *assumes* that the 1945 Simla conference did not collapse—and will not collapse. Instead, the "Simla conference" of the game will last about a year, with each public session occurring after a lapse of about two months. During this period, the British Governors General (or Viceroy), in consultation with whomever they wish, will address as best they can whatever developments transpire during the game. They may or may not choose to set up an interim government composed wholly or in part of Indian leaders.

Roles

The following is a list of the players and a summary of their public motives. (You must understand, of course, that—as in life—individual players may have secret motivations.) Appendix C, which includes the writings of some of these figures, provides a deeper perspective on their ideas. Diligent players will also undertake research on their own to uncover information about the other parties at the conference.

SUGGESTED ROLE DISTRIBUTION

Faculty may alter this distribution as suits their pedagogical purposes. Congress (INC) includes multiple roles. Every version of the game includes Maulana Azad, a Muslim, who is included on a separate line in the assignment table below. The Hindu leaders of the INC are divided into as many as six different roles: including Nehru, a secularist; a Hindu partisan (Brahman); one or two indeterminates, whose specialties are history or Hindu poetry; and a Bengali. The Muslim League, similarly, contains different roles: Ali Jinnah, a secularist; one or two indeterminates, whose specialties are history or Muslim poetry; and Sayyid Mawdudi, a radical Muslim cleric.

This table indicates the recommended role distribution based on class size.

CLASS SIZE	13	14	15	16	17	18	19	20	21	22	23	24	25	30	35
Governor(s) General	1	1	1	1	2	2	2	2	2	2	2	2	2	2	3
Gandhi A	1	1	1	1	1	1	1	1	1	1	1	1	1	2	2
Gandhi B	1	1	1	1	1	1	1	1	1	1	1	1	1	2	2
Indian National Congress															
Maulana Azad	1	1	1	1	1	1	1	1	1	1	1	1	1	1	2
Hindu: Nehru	1	1	1	1	1	1	1	1	1	1	1	1	1	2	2
Hindu: Brahman	1	1	1	1	1	1	1	1	1	1	1	1	1	1	1
Hindu: Historian/Poet			1	1	1	1	1	1	1	2	2	2	2	2	2
Hindu: Bengali							1	1	1	1	1	1	1	1	1
Muslim League															
Ali Jinnah	1	1	1	1	1	1	1	1	1	1	1	1	1	2	2
Sayyid Mawdudi	1	1	1	1	1	1	1	1	1	1	1	1	1	1	2
Muslim: Historian/Poet				1	1	1	1	2	2	2	2	2	2	2	2
Non-Factional															
Pres. Hindu Mahasabha	1	1	1	1	1	1	1	1	1	1	1	1	1	1	2
Dr. Ambedkar	1	1	1	1	1	1	1	1	1	1	1	1	1	1	2

Tara Singh, Sikh	1	1	1	1	1	1	1	1	1	1	2	2	2	2
Communist Party of India	1	1	1	1	1	1	1	1	1	2	2	2	2	2
Nizam of Hyderabad	1	1	1	1	1	1	1	1	1	1	1	1	1	1
Hari Singh, Maharaja of Kashmir	G	G	G	G	G	1	1	1	1	1	1	1	1	1
Rural Village Leader		1	1	1	1	1	1	1	2	2	2	2	3	4	4

NOTE: In classes with 17 or fewer players, the Gamemaster will also play the role of Hari Singh, Maharaja of Kashmir.

BRITISH GOVERNOR(S) GENERAL (VICEROY)

The British Governors General, having been summoned to succeed Lord Wavell somewhat hastily, cannot be assumed to possess perfect knowledge of the situation in India. As recent arrivals, they need to be appraised of each group's requests and objectives. To that end, the Governors General will devote the initial public sessions of the conference to hearing and discussing everyone's views.

(**Advisory:** All Simla participants should listen to these statements attentively and read all position papers carefully. The instructor will likely arrange for publication of most presentations [on some class-restricted website.])

The British have publicly proclaimed that their mission is to accomplish Indian independence and broker an equitable settlement that will allow Great Britain to withdraw from India honorably. Prime Minister Winston Churchill, who has ultimate power over his Viceroy(s), has made no secret of his wish to retain some vestige of India as the remaining "jewel" in the (somewhat tarnished) crown of British imperialism. At the very least, he doubtless has requested that a post-independence India remain within the British Commonwealth, the trade and cultural alliance composed of former colonies. The Prime Minister (Gamemaster) has the power to remove the Viceroy(s) and name a new one.

In addition to hosting the Simla conference, the Governors General control the civil and military bureaucracies that run India. They can order the arrest and imprisonment of nearly anyone on virtually any pretext. They can also outlaw organizations, direct the movement of military forces and police units, and otherwise issue orders to all agencies. They can do so publicly, by making announcements (and posting them on the website); or they can proceed in private, through communiqués to the Gamemaster (who will also function as the colonial bureaucracy—slowly, perhaps even inefficiently, but in accordance with the directions of the Governors General).

MEMBERS OF THE INC: THE CONGRESS PARTY

Since its founding in 1885, the Indian National Congress (INC, or Congress) has spearheaded the campaign for Indian independence from Great Britain. It is safe to assume that all members of Congress lose if, at the end of the game, India has not been granted independence and the British remain as an intrusive administrative, political, or military force on the subcontinent.

Although three-fourths of the population of India is Hindu, and an equivalent proportion of the Congress leadership is Hindu, Congress claims to represent all the peoples of India. Indeed, the president of Congress is Maulana Azad, a prominent Muslim. Congress leaders, moreover, have cultivated relationships among Sikh leaders and Dr. Ambedkar, the most visible spokesman for the Untouchables.

Congress proposes that Great Britain swiftly depart, allowing Congress to inherit administrative control of what has been the British Raj. The Congress leaders conceive of the transition as a turnkey operation: the British administrators will leave their posts, and Congress leaders will replace them. Congress would thus inherit a strong centralized governmental structure. Congress leaders further suggest that with the collapse of Japan, and with China embroiled in civil war between Communist and nationalist factions, a united India holds the promise of becoming one of the strongest nations in the world. Congress also dismisses claims by the independent princes that they should remain in power. Congress leaders hold that when the British leave India, the British treaties protecting such princes and upholding their sovereign powers will become null and void, in fact if not in law. Some princes have already announced their likely affiliation with Congress; others, such as the Nizam of Hyderabad, a Muslim, have insisted that their principality will retain their own independence even if the British depart.

Congress is not fully united. Among the Hindus within Congress, there are disputes over whether India should become a modern industrial power, as the Hindu Mahasabha proposes, or whether India should cling to its rural village traditions, as Gandhi advocates. Some want a future India to be modeled after the parliamentary democracy of Great Britain, while others, especially Jawaharlal Nehru, are drawn to socialistic and even communistic systems. Still others repudiate Western models and insist that any Indian government uphold traditional Indian (and especially Hindu) traditions. Some go so far as to demand the establishment of a new Hindu nation: Hindustan. Everyone recognizes that holding India together will be no easy matter. Muslims and other groups may seek to weaken Hindu confidence by underscoring the elements of division: the exclusion of the Untouchables from Hindu society; the vulnerability of the Sikhs; the independence of various principalities, and so on.

Congress is also divided between Hindus and "nationalist" Muslims, such as Maulana Azad. Azad, like Gandhi, wants Congress to become the umbrella organization representing all Indians. To that end, he does not want the INC to endorse explicitly Hindu causes, such as cow protection and Hindi as the national language.

Inseparable from the legacy of Congress is Mohandas Gandhi, the central figure in India's independence movement. Gandhi, though influential among Hindus and the Congress leadership, does not seek to create a secular, modernizing state along the lines of the Western nations (see Gandhi, below). This may cause some friction within Congress, as well as with the "westernizers" and "secularists" in Congress, of whom Jawaharlal Nehru (NAY-ROO) is most prominent.

Maulana Abdul Azad, the Muslim President of the INC, advocates the central unity of all Indians. He especially speaks for the 30 million or so Muslims who live in provinces where Hindus are in a large majority. (See Map B, Muslims as percent of total population c. 1930.) If India breaks into two separate nations, one predominantly Hindu and the other Muslim, the Muslims who remain in "Hindustan" will constitute a small minority, fearfully exposed to the huge Hindu majority. This is another reason why all Indians must learn to live together in a single Indian nation, or so Azad insists.

REPRESENTATIVES OF THE MUSLIM LEAGUE

The INC's claim that it speaks for all Indians has been sharply challenged by Muhammad Ali Jinnah and the Muslim League. Founded in 1906, the League contends that the overwhelming Hindu majority poses a danger to the Muslim minority. If Britain withdraws from India and the INC gains power, Congress leaders will likely install a democracy that ensures that the Muslim minority will possess little power, especially in the overall "national" government. The Hindu majority will elect nearly all of the leaders of the new nation, which could well be called Hindustan. The Muslim League scoffs at the INC's claim that it represents all of the peoples of India. Jinnah and other League leaders insist that Maulana Azad, the Muslim who is President of the INC, is merely a "show-boy"—the Muslim mask concealing Hindu aggression.

The Muslim League cites the increased politicization of Hindus, and the rise of the Hindu Mahasabha under the militant Savarkar during the twentieth century. Militant Hinduism ensures that the Hindu government will trample on the rights of Muslims and eventually suppress their religion and culture.

Leaders of the Muslim League believe that the days of cooperation are over. Jinnah, a leader of the League, had brokered a deal with the INC in 1916 (Lucknow Pact). But relations between Muslims and Hindus have deteriorated since then. In 1940, Jinnah, in his presidential address to the Muslim League at Lahore, demanded that India be divided into two nations:

"Islam and Hinduism are not religions in the strict sense of the word, but in fact are different and distinct social orders, and it is only a dream that the Hindus and Muslims can ever evolve a common nationality . . . . To yoke together two such nations under a single state . . . must lead to a growing discontent and final destruction of any fabric that may be so built up for the government of such a state."

As an alternative to a Hindu-dominated single Indian state, Jinnah and the Muslim League will likely propose the partition of India into a predominantly Hindu state and a predominantly Muslim state consisting of mostly Muslim areas in western India, east and south of the Indus River, and in eastern India, especially Bengal. The League proposes to call this Muslim state Pakistan.

Unclear at present is whether the League will propose that "Pakistan" be constituted as a secular state or as one based on Islamic principles, perhaps even on the strict precepts of Islamic law, or the *shariat*, as Sayyid Mawdudi proposes. The members of the League may differ on such matters, perhaps heatedly. But in all likelihood, the Muslims will seek to persuade the British of the need for a separate Muslim state, carved out of India.

Jinnah rejects Azad's notion that the Muslims who are left behind in "Hindustan" would be vulnerable. Jinnah has advanced what some call the "hostage theory": It holds that the Muslim majority could gain negotiating leverage by the fact that in Hindus would remain a vulnerable minority in Muslim-dominated Pakistan, just as Muslims would be a vulnerable minority in Hindu-dominated Hindustan. The Hindus could not abuse the Muslims in Hindustan because the Muslim-dominated government of Pakistan could retaliate against the Hindus in Pakistan. Dividing the subcontinent into two nations would help protect the minorities, or so Jinnah argues.

Although Jinnah and the Muslim League demand creation of Pakistan, some contend that they may be willing to endorse creation of a single Indian state in which the federal government possesses very limited powers. If Muslims can largely control what transpires in the Muslim provinces of a loosely federated Indian state, then affiliation with the Hindus would not be so terrible, or so some members of the Muslim League may assert. The Muslim League rejects entirely the leadership of some Muslims who have professed their support of the Congress and Congress's goal of a strong, united, and centralized India.

ADHERENTS OF MOHANDAS GANDHI

Mohandas Gandhi is a major spiritual, political, and diplomatic force. He is also one of the most complex leaders of the twentieth century. On the one hand, he enshrines the rural villages of traditional India, characterized by the economic self-sufficiency of local craftsmen and farmers, by adherence to traditional religious teachings (both Hindu and Muslim), and by social stability. He denounces Western concepts. Thus Gandhi refuses to wear manufactured textiles and instead can be seen in simple handwoven and handspun cotton clothes. "Real freedom for me will only come when we free ourselves of the dominance of Western education, Western culture, the Western way of living . . . Emancipation from this culture would mean real freedom for us," Gandhi declares. He also opposes modern medicine and foods. He reads the *Bhagavad Gita,* the classic Hindu text, every day. His vision of an ideal society in many ways corresponds with the Brahman conception of India.

On the other hand, some Indians denounce Gandhi for failing to promote Hindu goals. His ideal society appears to be at odds with traditional Hinduism, especially his pronouncements on behalf of the Untouchables (whom he identifies by the term *harijan*, "children of God") and his calls for accommodation with the Muslims. He champions nonviolence and seeks to defuse the tensions among ethnic groups, especially Muslims, Hindus, and Sikhs.

Gandhi's views are at times difficult to pin down. Moreover, although Gandhi has agreed to come to Simla, he has announced his intention of not attending the sessions because he is not at present an officer in the Congress party. However, leaders who espouse his principles—and sometimes his contradictory principles—will attend and present his views. And it is possible that Gandhi will himself decide to appear at the conference, or otherwise give speeches that will be heard throughout India. Gandhi retains great influence among Indians, especially those in Congress.

OSMAN ALI KHAN, NIZAM OF HYDERABAD

The Nizam—perhaps the richest man in the world—rules all of the state of Hyderabad in south central India. (See Map A, British India c. 1930.) Five-sixths of his subjects are Hindu. The Nizam is the most powerful and indisputably the richest of hundreds of Indian princes whose ancestors brokered treaties with the British to preserve their rule in return for special concessions to the British (revenue, police powers, foreign relations, etc.). Like many other princes, the Nizam now wants to preserve at least some semblance of his rule. During World War II he contributed to the British war effort several score warplanes. He doubtless worries that Indian independence will allow Hindus in the national capital to rule Hyderabad. He prefers that Hyderabad become a separate, and largely autonomous state within a loose Muslim (or perhaps Hindu) federation.

HARI SINGH, MAHARAJA OF KASHMIR

The Hindu counterpart of the Nizam of Hyderabad—a Muslim prince among a predominantly Hindu population—is Maharaja Hari Singh, the Hindu prince of Kashmir and Jammu, where three-fourths of the subjects are Muslim. Singh is the great-grandson of Maharaja Gulab Singh, founder of the state of Jammu and Kashmir. Like most other leaders of the hundreds of Princely States, Maharaja Hari Singh seeks to maintain some autonomy; yet he worries that if Kashmir is autonomous, the Muslim majority may seek to do away with him.

TARA SINGH, SIKH LEADER

The Sikhs (pronounced "six" or, sometimes in the West, "seeks") constitute less than 2 percent of the population of India, though they possess considerable economic influence in the Punjab. Sikhs transformed the Punjab into one of the most prosperous agricultural regions of India. The Punjab is a dry region, though five major rivers flow through it; Sikh ingenuity in devising irrigation, along with the skill of Sikh farmers, known as Jats, have made the Punjab the breadbasket of India.

Sikh means "disciple," a reference to the disciples of the Sikh guru Nanak (1469–1539). Nanak sought to "purify" Hinduism by purging it of polytheism and inegalitarianism (the caste system). The teachings of Nanak and his nine successors (together, the ten gurus) are recounted in the *Granth Sahib*, the sacred book of the Sikhs.

The popularity of Sikhism, as propounded by Nanak's fifth successor, the guru Arjan (1581–1606), threatened Mughal rule in northern India. He was captured and tortured by the Mughal emperor, but he refused to recant. Before he died, he got word to his son, Hargobind (1606–1645): "Sit fully armed on the throne and maintain the army to the best of your ability." Hargobind's tenure as sixth guru was characterized by his militarizing the Sikh religion and its society. Govind Singh (1675–1708), the tenth and final Sikh guru, declared that "the Sword is God and God is the sword!" Singh also founded the Khalsa, a religious brotherhood of Sikh males. (*Singh* means "lion," and all Sikh males are given this name.) Govind Singh also wrote a prayer, recited daily by Sikhs, to promote the cause: "The Khalsa shall rule; none who object to it shall exist. In humiliation the refractory shall submit and those who seek refuge shall be protected." By the eighteenth century, as the Mughal Empire declined, the Khalsa acquired influence over larger sections of the Punjab. But in the nineteenth century the British East India Company fought two bitter wars against the Sikhs, defeating them in 1849. The Punjab was then added to British India.

Because the Sikhs had proven to be formidable soldiers, the British East India Company recruited them to serve in the Company army, even allowing them to take their military oaths on Sikh scriptures and to wear the Sikh turban. Appreciative of British patronage, the Sikhs sided with the British during the Sepoy Mutiny of 1857. Though less than 2 percent of the population of India, the Sikhs accounted for one-fifth of Britain's armed forces. The Sikhs regarded themselves not as subject peoples to the British Raj but as "favorite sons of the Empress Mother," Queen Victoria.

Of the 1.2 million Indians who served in the British military during World War I, over 350,000 were from the Punjab—the center of Sikh power and influence. During the unrest following World War I, the Sikhs joined with Hindus and Muslims to seek Indian independence or autonomy. In 1922 Bhagat Singh, a young Sikh revolutionary, was convicted by a British court of political murder. When Singh and his accomplices were hanged, riots broke out in the Punjab, leaving hundreds dead. Gandhi expressed sadness at the violence but praised Bhagat Singh's bravery. "I would not flinch," he said, "from sacrificing even a million lives for India's liberty."

The Sikh representative(s) will doubtless propose an independent Sikh state in the Punjab. The Sikhs worry that their religion and culture will be extirpated if they are forced to live in a nation dominated by either Hindus or Muslims. The Sikhs, though long regarded as the finest soldiers in India, could hardly be expected to prevail in armed confrontation with either the Hindus or the Muslims of India.

Perhaps the Sikhs can persuade the British to grant them their own nation in the Punjab. Throughout the Raj, the Sikhs have been the staunchest supporters of Britain. Or perhaps the Sikhs will join Congress, hoping that their support for the majority party will persuade it to grant some autonomy to the Sikhs in the Punjab. Or perhaps the Sikhs will work with other minorities, perhaps even the Muslim League, to counterbalance the electoral power of the Hindus.

DR. B. R. AMBEDKAR, UNTOUCHABLE LEADER

Dr. B. R. Ambedkar, an Untouchable who received a PhD in economics from Columbia University, seeks to ensure that the departure of the British will result in political power for the Untouchables (identified as "Selected Castes" or, more precisely, "Out-Castes," in the bureaucratic euphemism of the day). He wants not only that Untouchables be treated decently, or accorded constitutional "rights," but that they acquire political power to ensure and preserve such rights.

A pivotal moment in Ambedkar's consideration of the problems of the Untouchables came in 1932. That year, in response to his requests, the British government agreed to "reserve" 71 seats in provincial executive councils for Untouchables. These "reserved" seats could only be held by Untouchables. Gandhi, however, was outraged at this fragmentation of the people of India into separate political entities. He thought this move was characteristic of a British policy of "dividing" India so as to ensure its subjugation. In protest, he went on a hunger strike. The British government, fearing that Gandhi might die and thereby plunge India into chaos, withdrew the proposal. Ambedkar assented to this decision (Poona Pact), but bitterly resented Gandhi's actions.

Ambedkar will likely propose that the British affirm the rights of Untouchables and ensure that, in all future legislative bodies and governmental administrations, Untouchables are accorded representation in proportion to their numbers in Indian society. The Untouchables, though constituting about one-sixth of the population of India—more than 70 million people— will likely lose nearly all elections because everywhere they constitute a minority, indeed, a despised minority. His goal is a type of political affirmative action, in which one-sixth of all legislative seats, administrative offices, and governmental positions are "reserved" explicitly for Untouchables, who are elected only by Untouchable voters ("separate electorates").

Ambedkar may approach Congress to support such measures. Yet there is the chance that in so large a group the needs of the Untouchables may be ignored. Moreover, many Hindus, especially Brahmans, believe that affirmative action on behalf of the Untouchables subverts the natural social order, undermines the social stability inherent in Hindu religious precepts, and threatens to plunge India into chaos. Some Hindu politicians may also insist that political strength depends on resisting the efforts of minorities to fracture the Hindu-dominated polity.

Thus Ambedkar may instead seek to join forces with the other important minorities in India. Insofar as the Untouchables are nearly as numerous as the Muslims, they would be an influential minority. But can any minority that opposes Congress expect to receive favorable or even fair treatment at the hands of Congress?

REPRESENTATIVE OF THE HINDU MAHASABHA

The Hindu Mahasabha, though founded in 1906 to protect Hindu cultural traditions and promote a Hindu state called Hindustan, did not attain prominence until the 1920s. By then, tensions between Hindus and Muslims had sparked frequent riots. Hindus were offended by the Muslims' public slaughter of cows; and Muslims became enraged when Hindu processions, drums pounding and trumpets blaring, marched past mosques during scheduled prayers. Fights ensued, often with heavy casualties. The Mahasabha's guiding force was—and is—V. D. Savarkar, who spent years in a British penal colony in the Andaman Islands on charges of terrorism. Savarkar was released in 1935, and since then he has become the leader of the movement. The Hindu Mahasabha has had an increasingly powerful effect on the leaders of Congress, who recognize that Mahasabites are capable of mobilizing, often in an instant, legions of militant followers. The Hindu Mahasabha functions as a cultural movement capable of inspiring radical Hindu politicians and also of influencing politicians in the Congress party. It opposes those who heap praise on Western institutions and embrace secular nostrums.

The Hindu Mahasabha vehemently denounces those who would tear "Mother India" into two separate nations. Although some of its adherents accept Gandhian nonviolence, the predominant ethos of the organization embraces the militant strategies of extremists such as Tilak and Savarkar. Unlike Gandhi, who endorses the values of the rural villages, the Hindu Mahasabha seeks to build a strong, modern (and thus industrial) nation. The Hindu Mahasabha, though intent on creating Hindustan, breaks with high-caste Hindus in its desire to break down caste barriers. A strong Hindu nation, the Mahasabha insists, requires that Hindus be united.

LEADER OF THE COMMUNIST PARTY OF INDIA

Communists view the ethnic tensions within India as part of the effort among British and American capitalists to disguise the class tensions at the heart of Indian society. The British divide the Indian people by keeping alive religious and ethnic tensions (the partition of Bengal in the early 1900s is an obvious example), thereby obscuring the British colonial (and capitalistic) subjugation of the workers and peasants of India. The leader of the Communist Party seeks to build a revolutionary movement that will topple the British imperialists and then the native ruling classes of India: the owners of factories and industries, and the wealthy landowners, *zamindars*, and other oppressors of the peasants.

The communist leader may follow the strategy outlined in *The Communist Manifesto* of Marx and Lenin (1848), or perhaps the guidance of Stalin, leader of the Soviet Union, or perhaps even Mao Zedong, leader of the communist party of China (*On New Democracy* [1940], available in English online).

In larger classes, there may be more than one Communist party in India. Whether they will agree on doctrine and strategy is unclear.

VILLAGE LEADERS OF RURAL (HINDU) INDIA

India has some 70,000 villages, most with from 1,500 to 2,500 people. Sometimes a village had a council, which chose a village leader who would provide guidance on various problems. Sometimes the leader was a *zamindar*, who advanced credit and possessed political power as a result of his economic power within the village. Sometimes communal leaders, articulating religious goals and agendas, became influential at the local level. There was no single model to determine how villages would respond to major challenges.

Nor was there a mechanism for village leaders to participate in the Simla conferences—and thus sit at the table and express their views. But any decision at Simla that endorsed a democratic solution would ultimately be determined by the villages of which India was largely composed. If, for example, Britain decides to relinquish India to the Indians, the likely outcome would be a continuation of the democratic processes that had been used in provincial elections. This means that the villages of India, the great majority of them predominantly Hindu, would elect the legislators and national leaders of a democratic Indian nation.

In the event of a national referendum on independence, or the election of a new Indian parliament, the "votes" of the village leaders will likely prove to be decisive.

Basic Game Rules

VICTORY OBJECTIVES

Each group has different victory objectives; even within groups, objectives differ. The rules of the game are flexible. Players will likely be pressured to compromise "their" views (as outlined in the "roles") but players who compromise too far will cease to be faithful to their core identity and constituency. If this happens, they will lose. Determining exactly when this point has occurred is the prerogative of the Gamemaster, whose judgment will be made after the game is over. This unseemly potency and subjectivity may offend. But life, too, unfolds in ways that defy our notions of fairness and objectivity.

TACTICS AND WEAPONS

Technical: Access to the Podium

All players will have the right to stand at the podium and be heard. The GM may interrupt the Governors General to ensure that this right is respected. If the Governors General persist in ignoring such requests, the GM may report their autocratic behavior to the Prime Minister in London, who may order their recall or dismissal. On the other hand, the British Governors General may choose to employ the GM as a police force to ensure decorum during the game. In certain circumstances, those in power may circumscribe players' access to the podium.

Indian leaders will try to win their objectives by persuading the Governors General to accede to their wishes, and then by persuading the others to go along with them. Persuasion may require additional inducements. Some possibilities (there are others) are indicated below.

Nonviolent Protests and "Direct Action"

The Muslim League, INC, Hindu Mahasabha, Sikhs, Communists, and/or Untouchables may at any time call upon their followers to respond to some decision, action, or policy. Any such proclamation must be made in class, in public, at the podium. A public call for "direct action" will likely trigger adherents in various villages and cities to rise up violently against specified religious or class rivals. The effectiveness of such protest/action is determined by how many leaders support such action and the numbers of their followers. If, for example, one member of the Muslim League calls for a "direct action" day against Congress, it will be less effective than an episode in which all three members of the ML call for such action. Similarly, a "direct action" initiated by the INC would be more effective than one initiated by the Muslim League, if only because the INC had far more adherents. The magnitude of the violence can be affected by actions of other parties as well. If, say, the entire Muslim League calls for a "direct action" day and the entire INC calls for protest on the same day, the likely result would be tens of thousands of casualties. On the other hand, some groups, especially the Gandhians, can help defuse violent tensions by deploring a "direct action" or a "nonviolent protest" before it gets underway. But no one knows, in advance, the outcome of any protest or direct action.

Remember: One can never anticipate all the ramifications of violence; the GM will input all the evidence pertaining to any situation in his master laptop computer (named Die-roll) and announce the outcome.

LIKELY ELECTORAL STRENGTH

In the event of a referendum, or a vote, the following percentages provide a very rough approximation of the religious distribution of British India.

Muslims	22%
Caste Hindus	58%
Untouchables	16%
Sikhs	2%
Christians, Jews	1%
Other	1%

Many Untouchables regard themselves as Hindus. Moreover, the above figures do not include a breakdown of the religious affiliations for the 600 princely states, of which Hyderabad and Kashmir are the largest. Most of the rulers of these states insist that they are not part of British India and thus are exempt from any decisions the British may broker with Indian leaders, such as the INC and the Muslim League.

It is wrong to assume, moreover, the all Hindus or Muslims will vote the same way, or that religion is the sole force in determining electoral outcomes. The Communist Party, for example, regards religion as an "opiate of the masses"; and some leaders of both the Indian National Congress and the Muslim League seek to create governments that are secular.

"Reserved Seats" Versus "Separate Electorates"

In the 1930s, the British introduced the concept of reserved seats in provincial legislatures for specific minorities, such as Untouchables, Muslims, and Sikhs. That is, if Untouchables constituted fifteen percent of the population of a province, then fifteen percent of the seats would be "reserved" for Untouchables. (In fact, sometimes the number of reserved seats were the product of political negotiations rather than demographic percentages.) This meant that in a 100-person legislature, fifteen of the seats could only be held by Untouchables, which would ensure their representation.

But this raised another practical problem. If voters who were not themselves Untouchables could vote to choose the Untouchable representatives, there was a chance that a large number of high-caste Hindu voters could choose "their" Untouchables, and thus prevent the real Untouchables from having meaningful representation. The same was true of other minorities.

So advocates of Untouchables, Muslims, Sikhs, and other minorities also demanded that on entering polling places, the "reserved" minorities would cast ballots in separate boxes. That is, only Untouchables could vote for the reserved Untouchable candidates; and only Muslims could vote for the reserved Muslim candidates.

Dr. Ambedkar will likely demand such an electoral policy for Untouchables; Gandhi will vehemently oppose it: to give the Untouchables separate ballots and representatives would be to institutionalize their separation from Indian society.

Electoral Simplicity

Literacy in India is very low. If there is to be a referendum of all adults (male and female), the issues must be simplified and converted to visual symbols. No one can expect all voters to read a paragraph or even a sentence. A referendum vote on cow protection, for example, could show two symbols: one, a cow; another, a cow with an X over it. A vote on partition, similarly, could show a symbol of one nation; another of two nations.

British election officials have had experience in conducting elections, most recently the 1937 election for provincial legislators. Any election or referendum might require their expertise (perhaps with the help of the Gamemaster).

FUNDAMENTAL CONSIDERATIONS

Players will inevitably be occupied with technical issues of constitution-making and government creation. But those who are most successful will take on the biggest issue—the meaning of nationality—and devise a coherent conception, consistent with their victory objectives, and relate it persuasively to the rest of the class. The technical issues will likely fall in place if the overall argument is persuasive.

WRITTEN ASSIGNMENTS

Each player's role sheet indicates their particular writing assignments. Most players will submit two papers; the first is due when students make presentations to the Governors General. The Governors General will then present a proposal for the future government of India, along with an explanation of their reasoning. Other players will then prepare second papers in response to the British proposal. The second paper will likely be an essay either in support of the Governors' framework, a request to modify it, or a political document soliciting public opinion in relation to a nationwide referendum or election of parliament. Groups, or multi-member factions, should coordinate their submissions to ensure that they have something substantive to say at every session.

Glossary

Adi Granth scripture of Sikhs, based on the teachings of Guru Nanak, compiled in the early 1600s

ahimsa nonviolence

Anandamath a novel by Bankim Chandra Chatterji

"Bande Mataram" "Salutation to the Mother," a song, originally about Bengal, for Hindu India

Brahman status category of highest priestly caste in classic Sanskrit literature

charkha the spinning wheel, a symbol of the artisanal cotton-based economy of Gandhi

Dalit "down-trodden," a modern term used by Untouchables to describe their community

dharma a set of specific moral and religious obligations in Hinduism

harijan "children of God," Gandhi's term for Untouchables

hartal a general strike, including the closing of shops, usually called to initiate a political protest

hindutva Hindu essence or equivalency

Indian Civil Service (ICS) the bureaucracy of colonial India, largely staffed by Indians under direction of British

jagidir a Mughal retainer who had been given the right to assess and collect tax on a particular parcel of land (*jagir*)

Jat a peasant or farming community in northern India

jihad a holy war; an effort to attain perfection, in Islam

karma the concept of reincarnation, where future births are based on one's actions in his or her current life

khadi a handwoven cotton cloth, often associated with Gandhi

Khilafat (caliphate) the office of the caliph, the spiritual leader of all Muslims within the Ottoman Empire

Mahabharata a classic Hindu text of ancient India

Maharaja great ruler, or king (Hindu)

Mahatma "great soul," applied to Gandhi

mullah an Islamic religious leader

nizam prince, or ruler (Muslim)

Pandit a Hindu religious scholar; the title given to Jawaharlal Nehru of Congress

Quaid "great leader," title for Mohammad Ali Jinnah

R.I.N. the Royal Indian Navy

raj a kingdom

rupee the main unit of Indian currency

sabha an association

sati Indian funeral practice in which a woman commits suicide, often by immolation on the funeral pyre of her husband

satyagraha "way of truth," or "truth force," Gandhi's strategy of nonviolent confrontation

Sikh a "disciple," specifically referring to followers of Guru Nanak

swadeshi "of our own country," a phrase often applied to a preference for buying India-made goods

swaraj self–rule

varna literally, "color" in Hindi, but usually implying "caste," or the hierarchical arrangement of social groups

Appendix A: Hinduism and the *Bhagavad Gita*

Westerners have long been struck by the pervasive influence of religion in Indian life. When Mark Twain visited India in the 1890s, he referred to it as "the home of a thousand religions and two million gods." His words echoed those of Basavanna, a twelfth-century Indian poet who complained of the proliferation of deities in south India: "Gods, gods, there are so many, there's no place left for a foot." Swami Vivekananda, who introduced many westerners to Indian religion in the 1890s, contrasted the spirituality of India with the materialism of the West. India, he declared, "is the land to which every soul that is wending its way Godward must come." The evident spirituality of the Indians in contrast with the West constituted a cornerstone in the thought of Mohandas Gandhi, who was called "Mahatma" (great soul).

Yet not all Indians endorsed India's religiosity. Jawaharlal Nehru, a key figure in the twentieth-century Indian independence movement (and in this game), complained that religion stood in the way of progressive change. "Religion in India," he wrote, "has not only broken our backs but stifled and killed all originality of thought and mind." The Communist Party of India, following Karl Marx, denounced religion as the "opiate of the masses."

Four religions are indigenous to India: Hinduism, Buddhism, Jainism, and Sikhism. All share certain fundamental assumptions: The first concerns the concept of *reincarnation,* or *samsara,* the idea that all living things will die but will be reborn again in some form.

Another major concept is *karma,* a word for which there is no real translation. It conveys the idea that all actions—mental, emotional, physical—must have consequences that lead to rebirth. Good *karma* is a cosmic benefaction or gift that will redound to a person's future benefit; conversely, bad behavior will incur bad *karma,* a train of baleful consequences that will dog a person's footsteps in the future (whether in this life or another one).

A third assumption is embodied in another word for which there is no ready equivalent, *dharma,* which refers to the moral obligations that come with birth and that are not imposed by any deity but result from one's own actions in previous lives. *Dharma* refers to that which is and which should be. Good people fulfill their *dharma.* The concept of *dharma* is sometimes illustrated by the story of the devout Hindu who rescues a scorpion that is drowning in a pool of water. It bites him. When it again slips into the pool, the holy man again rescues it—and again is bitten. "Why," a companion asks, "did you pick it up when you knew it would bite you?" The holy man replied, "A scorpion's *dharma* is to bite; my *dharma* is to save; each of us does what we must." To ignore one's *dharma*—say, by marrying outside of one's appropriate social group or caste—is to violate deep-seated cultural traditions and family values and to undermine the cosmic order.

A fourth concept is *moksha,* a liberation from the cycle of birth and rebirth, a transcendence of mortal existence.

These concepts—*samsara, karma, dharma,* and *moksha*—are part of a worldview that seems, from very ancient times, to have pervaded Indian thought and culture. They are expressions of a social as well as religious character.

Some Indians claim that Hinduism is not a religion but many forms of belief and practice loosely linked together. It has no single authoritative scripture but rather a multitude of sacred texts; it has no identifiable historical figure as founder, no creedal statements to summarize its beliefs, and no institutional structure to guarantee conformity. Hinduism has absorbed ideas from innumerable faiths, religious guides and philosophies. Despite the immense diversity of its content, the term "Hinduism" is used by Hindus themselves, not only in English but also in Indian languages, to differentiate themselves from adherents to other religions.

From 2000 to 600 B.C.E., a vast literature was produced that became the charter documents of Hinduism, the oldest of which are the *Vedas*. They describe the rites and ceremonies by which Hindu priests—*Brahmans*—performed sacrifices to maintain the cosmic order. Over time Brahmanism was challenged by practitioners of other faiths, such as Buddhism and Jainism, who emphasized devotional beliefs and practices of non-elites. Around 500 B.C.E., these new concepts were fused with the old: Increasingly, Hinduism held that life itself was a form of sacrifice, a subduing of the self to help preserve the cosmic order.

In this literature, the priests, or Brahmans, have a vital role as religious specialists, because they alone had the knowledge for the correct performance of the rituals that maintain the cosmic order through sacrifices to the gods. In addition to the priests, Vedic Hinduism refers to a second kind of religious specialist: the *guru*. He or she—for the guru can be either man or woman—is a spiritual guide who has found the way to truth and is able to help others. Spiritual guides are numerous throughout all levels of Indian society.

In modern India, the appeal to return to "Hindu values" usually refers to the way of life that was articulated by Brahmanical Hinduism. The ideal of the good society that emerges in the literature can be summarized under two grand concepts. The first of these is of society divided into four great divisions, or *varnas,* with each class being bound to the others by reciprocal duties, creating a harmonious society. There is no historical evidence that such a society ever existed in reality, but the idea has had immense appeal through the ages, with Mahatma Gandhi being an influential exponent of a modernized version. The other, closely related, is that the good person is one who finds the meaning of life in following his or her *dharma.*

The four traditional *varnas* are: Brahmans (priests), Khsatriyas (kings and warriors), Vaisyas (common people), and Sudras (servants). Within these varnas are thousands of particular occupational subdivisions (*jatis),* many of which provide specific guidance on work, marriage, and behavior. A person's proper, rightful role, specific to his caste, is known as his *dharma.*

THE BHAGAVAD GITA

While the *Vedas* are the foundational texts of Hinduism, perhaps the most important single text was the *Bhagavad Gita,* "The Song of the Divine One." It was added to the *Mahabharata,* the ancient epic text of Hinduism, around 500 B.C.E. The *Bhagavad Gita* consists chiefly of a conversation between Arjuna, a warrior prince, and Krishna, his charioteer and guide. It occurred during the Mahabharata War, fought at the dawn of civilization, when two great armies converged at Kuruksheka (near Panipat), on the plain north of Delhi that slopes toward the foothills of the Himalayas. Arjuna commands the army of the Pandava clan, which is legally entitled to rule; the opposing army is commanded by a rival clan that has usurped the Pandava kingdom.

What follows is as brief chapter summary:

CHAPTER 1

Dhrita-Rasthra, the blind king whose son, Duryodhana, has wrongfully seized the Pandava throne, asks his chief minister, Sanjaya, to explain what is happening on the battlefield. Sanjaya has magical powers that allow him to see and hear what is going on in the Pandava camp. Sanjaya describes how Arjuna, the foremost Pandava general, has asked his charioteer, Krishna, to drive to a position between the two armies. Sanjaya relays the conversation between Arjuna and Krishna, a conversation that constitutes much of the *Bhagavad Gita*.

Arjuna tells Krishna that he is anxious about the impending battle. He despairs of the bloodshed; among his concerns is the fact that any war results in the death of husbands and fathers and thus destroys families. An "unrighteous disorder prevails," which means that "the women sin and are impure." Widows and unmarried women may be forced to have sexual relations with men outside of their caste. This causes a "disorder of castes, social confusion." Implicit is the assumption that all men must uphold *dharma*—the proper ordering of society—but war, by shattering marriages and families, nearly always undermines social order.

Arjuna, dejected, puts down his bow and arrow.

Discussion: The opening scene of the *Bhagavad Gita* describes two armies preparing for war, accompanied by the roar of conch-shells, the rumble of war drums, the "stirring sound" of cymbals and trumpets, and horns filling the sky "with a fearful thunder." Why this conversation was set on a battlefield has long puzzled scholars. In the twentieth century, militant Hindus regarded this as proof that Hinduism was an activist faith, focused on the affairs of this world: good Hindus do **not** retreat to a monastery and renounce the world. Even warfare was appropriate for a just cause. Gandhi disagreed: He regarded the battlefield scene as the most dramatic context possible to illuminate a discussion of how one must do his duty in the world; all men must decide whether to fight injustice or surrender to it.

CHAPTER 2

Krishna tells Arjuna to "be a man." But Arjuna remains despondent. Then Krishna claims to give voice to the word of God. What follows is one of the most profound philosophies of the ancient world—or of any subsequent one: "The unreal never is: the Real never is not." The world of the senses, which appears to be "real," is in fact an illusion; on the other hand, a person's spirit, which cannot be seen or felt, is real, because it exists forever. Death can only come to the physical realm, a world of impermanence. Death cannot touch the spiritual realm. Physical death matters little because all will be "born again and again, and again and again".

If Arjuna slays his enemies, he kills no one, because no one can kill a soul; and the souls of the slain will find expression within new bodies through reincarnation. Bodies, which are of the physical world, are ultimately inconsequential. Arjuna is unpersuaded. Krishna adds another argument: Arjuna's *dharma* is that of a warrior (*kshatriya*). This obliges him to fight. Indeed, a failure to fight will not only be regarded as an act of cowardice, but it will also constitute a "transgression" of his caste obligation. One never sins by doing one's duty; and Arjuna's duty—his *dharma*—is to fight. He can never sin by adhering to his *dharma*.

But Arjuna's doubts persist. To drive a sword through the heart of a beloved teacher or kinsman seems sinful. Krishna counters that in all actions, a person's motivation matters more than the action itself. If people monitor their motivations, and perform proper actions according to a spirit of sacrifice totally uninfluenced by passionate desire, then they will do no wrong. Conversely, a farmer seemingly does his duty by pulling weeds; but if he dreams of selling his produce to make money, then he has sinned; if, however, he works in a spirit of sacrifice, with no regard for profit or material comfort, but instead seeks only to alleviate hunger (the *dharma* of all farmers), then he has done good.

Discussion: This concept differs profoundly from some Western religious beliefs. Catholics and many fundamentalist protestants similarly call on people to do "good works," but these good works (though often of a selfless character—caring for lepers, for example) redound to the doer's ultimate benefit: they lead to eternal salvation. Conceivably, "good works" in Hinduism may generate good *karma*, but the route to the Infinite Being in Hinduism is far less direct. What matters more than one's actions are the motivations behind them.

Hinduism, moreover, sees benefit in transcending the "unreal" world of the here and now, of the everyday senses. A virtuous person must never be so caught up in the affairs of the world that he loses sight of the eternal spirituality that transcends that world.

Chapter 3

The chapter explores a seeming contradiction. A person must do what is prescribed by his *dharma*. This inevitably binds him to the world. If one's *dharma* is to cultivate crops, then one must satisfy the needs of hungry people. But if he renounces desire, does this not entail a renunciation of his *dharma*, too?

Discussion: The issue is difficult; Hindus debate it at length. But while Buddhism explicitly embraces renunciation of the world—the monks who retreat to remote monasteries and indulge a life of contemplation are examples—this chapter of the *Gita* advances an alternative principle—of *karmayoga*—which calls on Hindus to embrace action: "Action is greater than inaction." People are enmeshed in a social world, defined by caste and *dharma;* the castes have responsibilities to their community that cannot be evaded. Hindus must not seclude themselves in monasteries and devote themselves to the contemplation of the Infinite.

Chapter 4

Because Hindus often worship different deities, Hinduism is sometimes regarded as polytheistic. But this chapter explains how the various deities of Hindu devotion are expressions of the Divine One.

Krishna explains that he has taught his message to the Sun; Arjuna declares this to be impossible, because Krishna is not as old as the Sun. Krishna now reveals that, as Krishna, he is an incarnation of the Eternal God: "He who knows my birth as God," Krishna adds, "goes no more from death to death." "For many are the paths of men"—Krishna adds, perhaps a reference to the worship of multiple deities—"but they all in the end come to me."

Those who believe in Krishna will be "made pure by the fire of wisdom." But devotion does not suffice. The remainder of the chapter reiterates the main point of the previous chapter:

In the bonds of works I am free . . . because in them I am free from desires. The man who can see this truth, in his work he finds his freedom . . . This was known by men of old times, and thus in their work they found liberation. Do thou therefore thy work in life in the spirit that their work was done.

Chapter 11

This chapter offers further affirmation that Krishna encompasses all deities: "I am the One source of all". The *Qur'an,* the holy book of the Muslims, includes similar language: Allah is the one and only God; but while Muhammad destroys the idols that represent the other gods of the Arabs, Krishna explains that he is the manifestation of all gods: "all the gods come from me." The other gods are not false; they are merely incomplete manifestations of Himself.

In the *Qur'an* Allah informs Muhammad that Allah causes all actions; when Muhammad's army wins a battle, Allah explains that Allah ensured victory. Similarly, in the *Gita* Krishna explains that Arjuna will prevail in the battle even if he does not lift a weapon because "I have come here to slay [your enemies]."

> Through the fate of their Karma I have doomed them to die: be though merely the means of my work.

In Chapter 11 Arjuna, trembling, bows in adoration. Krishna then reveals himself in his Infinite Form, "made of light" and "never seen by man before."

> If the light of a thousand suns suddenly arose in the sky, that splendor might be compared to the radiance of the Supreme Spirit.

Krishna then reappears in his human form. Arjuna yearns to again glimpse "thine own four-armed form, thou of arms infinite, Infinite Form."

Krishna explains that only Arjuna has seen him so: "Not by the *Vedas,* or an austere life, or gifts to the poor, or ritual offerings can I be seen as thou has seen me. Only by love can men see me, and know me, and come unto me."

HINDUISM, UNTOUCHABILITY, AND CASTE

The fate of the Untouchables, who comprised about one-sixth of the population of the Indian subcontinent, constituted a major political issue in 1945. At that time, the term "untouchables" then referred to any of a wide range of low-caste Hindu groups as well as others outside of the caste system.

Untouchability was partly defined by occupation: those who worked in activities that were regarded by Hindus as "impure," such as those involved with killing (butchers, fishermen), with working on the bodies of dead things (tanning, leatherworking), or with human bodily emanations—feces, urine, sweat (sweepers, clotheswashers). Those tribes that ate meat, similarly, were regarded as polluted—and thus as untouchable.

Untouchables were commonly regarded by orthodox Hindus as deeply polluted. Untouchables were excluded from most Hindu temples, schools, and even village wells. Sometimes they were obliged to live in segregated districts outside of towns and villages. In parts of India, high caste Hindus were thought to be polluted by contact with Untouchables—or even by merely seeing them. This obliged Untouchables to shout out their presence, or to do their work in public—sweeping streets, for example—at nighttime. High-caste Hindus who were "polluted" by their exposure to Untouchables were obliged to undergo rituals of purification.

British governors, to avoid the pejorative associations of the term "Untouchables," referred to them as Unscheduled Castes (in opposition to the four regular *varnas,* or castes). Gandhi complained that the British insistence on categorizing Indians, especially in census enumerations, helped cement the concepts and build walls between the India peoples. Gandhi, who fought to improve the lives of the Untouchables, identified them as *"harijans"*—children of God. Dr. B. R. Ambedkar, an Untouchable who earned a doctorate at Columbia University, sought to empower the Untouchables politically. (The writings of Gandhi and Ambedkar, found in Appendix C of this game book and in other writings, are central to this game.)

The extent to which Untouchability was a fundamental belief of Hinduism was a source of considerable debate. The concept certainly is mentioned in the *Vedas* and other religious texts; but its centrality to Hinduism was disputed.

The relevance of the caste system to Indian politics was also a source of considerable dispute. In *The Discovery of India,* Jawaharlal Nehru, a leader of the Indian National Congress, observed:

> Almost everyone who knows anything at all about India has heard of the caste system; almost every outsider and many people in India condemn it or criticize it as a whole.

But while he was a bitter foe of untouchability, and assumed that modernizing economic forces would bring about its end, he was nevertheless unsure of what that would mean for the future.

> The conflict is between two approaches to the problem of social organization, which are diametrically opposed to each other: the old Hindu conception of the group being the basic unit of organization [caste, *dharma*], and the excessive individualism of the west, emphasizing the individual above the group.

In a speech in Madras in 1921, Gandhi himself defended the caste system, whose highest culmination was found in the Brahmans:

> I have not a shadow of a doubt that Hinduism owes all to the great traditions that the Brahmans have left for Hinduism. They have left a legacy for India, for which every Indian, no matter to what varna he might belong, owes a deep debt of gratitude. . . . I would therefore urge—a non-Brahman myself—all non-Brahmans to whom my voice may reach that they will make a fundamental error if they believe that they can better their position by decrying Brahmanism (*The Hindu,* April 9, 1921).

In his newspaper *Young India,* Gandhi had earlier endorsed the principles outlined by Krishna in the *Bhagavad Gita* concerning caste. Gandhi believed that "the law of heredity is an eternal law and any attempt to alter that law must lead us, as it has before led, to utter confusion" (Gandhi, *Collected Works,* Vol. 19, pp. 83–84). Appalled by the industrial squalor and tenements of European manufacturing cities, Gandhi regarded the hereditary occupations of Hinduism as an antidote to class warfare and competition; caste, too, functioned as a self-governing system that enforced social norms and preserved social order, reducing the need for the harsh coercive powers (and vast standing armies) of the national states that were looming so menacingly over Europe in the twentieth century.

Appendix B: Muhammad and the *Qur'an*

ISLAM AND THE QUR'AN

"Islam" is an Arabic word whose linguistic roots—*s-l-m*—mean both submission and peace, as in the familiar greeting, "*salaam.*" Islam consequently is a religion that asks its adherents, called Muslims, to submit completely to the will of Allah, creator and ruler of the universe; Muslims use the word *Allah* in much the same way that Jews and Christians use the word God.

According to Islam, Allah revealed His intentions to many prophets, including Noah, Moses and Jesus. But Allah chose Muhammad, a seventh-century Arab trader, to be His final prophet. In 610 A.D., Muhammad received his first revelation from Allah. Over the next two decades Muhammad received 114 revelations. One revelation itself explained that Allah spoke to Muhammad "by suggestion, as if from behind a veil, or through a messenger sent and authorized by Allah to suggest what He pleases."

After the Prophet's death in 632, Muhammad's sayings were compiled into a single text called the *Qur'an* (sometimes spelled *Koran*), the sacred scripture of Islam; each revelation became a separate chapter, called *sura,* of the *Qur'an.*

The *suras* are arranged (mostly) with the longest first and then in descending order of length. This structure fractures both the chronological sequence of the revelations as well as the narrative order of events. Sayyid Mawdudi,[1] a major twentieth-century Islamic commentator (and a key figure in the early history of Pakistan), conceded that a stranger to the *Qur'an* will be baffled by its organization and structure: "He begins to feel that the *Qur'an* is a book without any order or interconnection between its verses or continuity of its subject." The *Qur'an* does not adhere to chronological order because it is not a work of history; it does not group its topics because it is not a work of philosophy. Instead, Mawdudi explained, a reader should accept from the outset that the *Qur'an* is "the only book of its kind in the whole world: that its literary style is quite different from that of all other books: that its theme is unique and that his preconceived notions of a book cannot help him understand the *Qur'an.*"[2]

The best way to understand the *Qur'an* is to listen to it, in Arabic, repeatedly, from beginning to end. Many Islamic scholars insist that the *Qur'an* cannot be translated. They speak of translations as attempts to convey surface meanings: the literal truth of the *Qur'an* is inseparable from the poetic Arabic in which it was originally expressed. One of the first translators described the *Qur'an* in the original Arabic as "an immutable symphony, the very sound of which moves men to tears and ecstasy."[3]

---

1. Mawdudi is also spelled Maududi or Maudoodi.
2. Sayyid Abul A'la Maududi, *The Meaning of the Quran,* Vol 1. (Lahore, 1967), p. 8.
3. Muhammad Marmaduke Pickthall, *The Meaning of the Glorious Koran: and Explanatory Translation* (New York: American Library, 1953), p. 11. An Englishman who became a convert, he insisted that only believers could translate it with any degree of accuracy.

Yet those who do not speak Arabic must rely on translations; and, as Sayyid Mawdudi (a key figure in modern Muslim doctrine) observed, the *Qur'an* presupposes that readers know the story of Muhammad: "One cannot understand fully many of the topics discussed in the *Qur'an* unless one is acquainted with the background of their revelation." Thus Allah "revealed the *Qur'an* piecemeal to meet the requirements of the [Islamic] Movement in its different stages."[4] What follows, then, is a brief account of Muhammad's life, accompanied by pertinent sections (*suras*) of the *Qur'an*.

THE EARLY LIFE OF MUHAMMAD: 570–609

Muhammad was born around 570 in Mecca, on the western edge of the Arabian Desert. His father died before his birth, and Muhammad's grandfather took charge of the boy. Because city life was regarded as unhealthful, the infant was sent to a wet nurse from a nomadic tribe, and Muhammad spent some of his infancy in the desert. At six, Muhammad's mother died; and at eight, his grandfather died as well.

Muhammad was then placed under the protection of an uncle, Abu Talib, leader of the Hashim clan. The Hashim were one of the larger kinship networks in the Quraysh tribe that dominated Mecca. Muhammad was trained in archery, swordsmanship and wrestling. He apparently traveled on some trading ventures with Abu Talib.

At this time Mecca was a major mercantile center for the camel caravans from Ethiopia, the Mediterranean, and Yemen. Part of Mecca's appeal was that it was home of the *Ka'aba,* a cube-shaped shrine dedicated to the highest god of the Arabs and surrounded by statues of another 360 gods. The Quraysh tribe supervised the *Ka'aba,* ensuring the safety of all pilgrims and traders.

But the community values that characterized Arab tribes in the desert were being eroded by the circumstances of urban life. Arab traders and bankers, striving for riches, concentrated on their own advancement and neglected their obligations to the tribe. As a young man Muhammad, who lacked the resources to engage in trade independently, perhaps pondered the materialism that eroded traditional Arab values.

On a trading journey around 595, Muhammad was charged with looking after the merchandise of a wealthy widow, Khadijah. She was impressed with him and proposed marriage. He accepted. The couple had six children. Her wealth provided him with the wherewithal to join the mercantile elite of Mecca.

THE FIRST REVELATION (610 A.D.)

In 610, Muhammad and his family went on a retreat to the mountains outside Mecca. While sightseeing at a cave, Muhammad was visited by an immense presence—he later identified it as the angel Gabriel—who instructed him to "Recite." Muhammad replied that he knew not how.

---

4. Maududi, *Meaning*, p.14.

Then the angel embraced him and said, "You are the Messenger of Allah," and commenced conveying verses of a holy book called the *Qur'an*—"the recitation."

Sura 96 (Recite)

1. *Recite in the name of your Lord, who created Man from a clot of blood*

2. *Recite! Your Lord is Most Bountiful,*

3. *Who taught man the art of writing with a pen*

4. *Taught man what he knew not.*

5. *Man errs*

6. *In thinking himself his own master:*

7. *For all things return to your Lord.*

Afterwards Muhammad could hardly believe what had happened in the cave, and said so to his family. But Khadijah and others offered reassurances. Eventually Muhammad came to understand that Allah had selected him as a prophet, like Moses and Jesus; Muhammad's task was to convey Allah's new messages to mankind. But while Allah had sent previous prophets to the Jews and Christians, Muhammad was the first Arab prophet; and Allah's message was to be conveyed in Arabic. Usually the revelations came from a male angel. But sometimes, Muhammad explained, the revelations came "like the reverberations of a bell." Increasingly the revelations were conveyed directly to Muhammad's heart.

THE REVELATION OF 615

Muhammad initially shared his revelations with only his family and a small group of acquaintances. They performed the prescribed prayers, bowing and touching their foreheads to the ground, and otherwise submitting to Allah's will. But these actions—especially the abject prostration of the Muslims during prayer—offended the sensibilities of many members of the Quraysh tribe. Some of them regarded these new practices as blasphemous.

In 615 Muhammad received a new revelation. He must proselytize more broadly: he was to spread the word of Allah to "his nearest relations"—a reference, clearly, to the whole Hashim clan. He was to warn them of the error of their ways:

Sura 26 (Warn your Nearest Relations)

213. *So call on no other god besides Allah . . . lest you end up among those who suffer His punishment.*

214. *Warn the members of your family,*

215. *Be kind to those who believe in you.*

216. *But if they disobey you, then say: "Surely I am not responsible for what you do."*

Muhammad's initial attempt to warn his family misfired. He had invited the men of the Hashim clan to a meal whose simplicity echoed the abstemious message of the *Qur'an.* Then he appealed to the gathering to convert to Islam. Few did so, and some ridiculed him and his revelations; these insults were a recurrent theme in the Meccan revelations—those he received when he lived in Mecca.

But the vehemence of his critics was in part a response to the fact that Muhammad posed a powerful threat to the Meccan trading elite. Young people were especially drawn to Muhammad's criticisms of the materialism and selfishness of Meccan society; and nearly all Arabs were impressed with the beauty and power of the Arabic of Muhammad's revelations.

THE ATTACK ON POLYTHEISM: 616

That Muslims were obliged to submit completely to Allah implied that they owed no obligations to the traditional deities worshiped by Arab peoples. Muhammad's attack on the traditional gods infuriated the leaders of the Quraysh. Yet his critics begrudgingly acknowledged Muhammad's powerful influence upon the young, so some Qurayshi leaders approached Muhammad with a compromise: they would endorse Allah and Islam if Muhammad would accept some of the traditional gods, especially the three goddesses of Mecca (Al-Lat, Al-Uzza, and Manat), as lesser deities ruled by Allah. Muhammad was perhaps tempted by this compromise:[5] (Sura 17: They Nearly Lured You Away from Our Revelations).

> 73. *Indeed, they [the Meccans] nearly lured you [Muhammad] away from Our revelations, so that you might invent some other scripture in Our name. Then they would have taken you for a friend.*

> 74. *Had We [again, Allah] not enabled you to stand firm, you might have inclined a little bit towards them.*

But then Muhammad came down emphatically against idolatry.

> ### Sura 53 (The Goddesses of Mecca are but Names)

> 18. *Did you ponder Al-Lat and Al-Uzza*

> 19. *And Manat, the third [the three pagan goddesses of Mecca, daughters of god]?*

> 20. *They are but names which you and your fathers have invented:*

> 21-24. *Allah has given them no powers.*

The point was hammered home in *Sura 112*, one of the shortest: (Sura 112 [Allah is the One God]).

---

5. This incident refers to one the most controversial issues surrounding the *Qur'an*. According to Al-Tabari, a ninth century Persian historian and important commentator on the *Qur'an*, Muhammad pondered adding two verses to *Sura 53*:18–19, which seemingly endorsed the three principal goddesses of Mecca: 18. Have you considered Al-Lat and Al-Uzza; and 19. and on Manat, the third [the three pagan goddesses of Mecca, daughters of God]?

Al-Tabari claimed that a wily Satan had tempted Muhammad into uttering these latter two verses, which some critics dubbed "the satanic verses." Karen Armstrong, in *Muhammad: A Biography of the Prophet* (1991), explained that Western critics err when they cite these passages as evidence that Muhammad was not receiving the word of God. The Christian conception of Satan—the ultimate source of evil in the world—differs from the Islamic conception, which regards Satan as a deficient genie who tempts and deceives mankind but does not bring about mankind's destruction. Muhammad's capacity to be "lured" by Satan underscores the importance of free will in Islamic thought (pp.112–115).

As Muhammad's group grew—perhaps approaching 100 followers—the leaders of the Quraysh put increasing pressure on Abu Talib, leader of the Hashim clan, to silence and punish Muhammad. Talib, though unpersuaded of Muhammad's revelations, refused to silence his nephew. More important, Talib persisted in declaring that Muhammad, as a son of the Hashim, was protected by the entire clan. Should any of his foes kill Muhammad, the Hashim would avenge his death.

Tensions mounted. When Muslims came into contact with other Quraysh, insults would fly. Sometimes scuffles escalated into riots. Vulnerable Muslims—slaves and the poor—lived in real danger, and Muhammad arranged for several score Muslim families to leave Mecca and settle in Abyssinia in North Africa, where they would fall under the protection of the local Christian ruler.

The organized exodus of large numbers of Muslims, including the children of well-to-do Qurayshi merchants, enraged the leaders of Mecca. On several occasions conspirators attempted to assassinate Muhammad but each time Allah intervened, or so Muhammad claimed. One would-be assassin, after overhearing a *sura,* put away his weapon and converted to Islam on the spot.

FLIGHT TO MEDINA: 622

In 619, Khadija, Muhammad's beloved wife, died. That same year, Abu Talib, Muhammad's uncle, protector, and head of the Hashim, fell ill and died. The new leader of the Hashim clan was Abu Lahab, Muhammad's staunchest enemy. Attacks on Muslims intensified, as did threats against Muhammad.

The next year, a group of Arabs were impressed by the Muslims and their new faith. They were from Medina, a fertile oasis about 200 miles north of Mecca. These Arabs converted to Islam and proposed that Muhammad and the Muslims join them in Medina, which was inhabited by Jewish and Arab farming tribes. In 622, Muhammad called on Muslims to make a *hijra*—an emigration—from Mecca to Medina. Compromise with the Quraysh was out of the question: the Muslims would go their own way.

The Quraysh, on the other hand, had refused to let the Muslims establish a rival source of power. Bloodshed seemed inevitable. The Qurayshi leaders had encouraged thugs to assassinate him and humiliate his followers. Should Muslims resist and, if so, should they respond with force?

Allah's response was emphatic:

Sura 22 (Jihad: Allah's Permission to Fight Injustice)

38. *Allah will defend believers; Allah does not love traitors.*

39. *Those who fight because they are wronged have permission to fight. Surely Allah will grant them victory—*

78. *Fight for the cause of Allah with the devotion due to Him. . . .*

"Fight for the cause of Allah"—the Arabic term is *jihad*—is a concept that has generated controversy.[6] It means either "armed action to achieve the will of Allah" or a more personal "striving to walk in

---

6. One who does *jihad* is a *mujahid*; the plural is *mujahideen.*

the path of Allah." The context of *Sura 22* makes it clear that *jihad* here means armed resistance to oppressors: "Permission is given to those who fight because they are wronged." Muslims would not require Allah's permission to follow His path, a task they were obliged to undertake.

For a time, Muhammad remained in Mecca, planning emigrations to Medina. In October 622, hundreds of Muslims trekked north to Medina. (The history of the Muslim era commences not with the birth of Muhammad or with his first revelations, but with the 622 *hijra* to Medina, the first concrete implementation of Allah's plan.) As Muslim merchants and shoppers disappeared from the markets and the streets of Mecca, the Quraysh became even angrier at Muhammad.

War was inevitable, but Muhammad knew that the Muslims would win. To that end, he obliged Muslims to take a "Pledge" of *jihad*. Such fighting within a tribe was almost without precedent. Allah provided Muhammad with clarifications on the nature of *jihad*: Muslims must fight evil-doers, especially those who drove the Muslims out of Mecca; but Muslims must also show "kindness" to those who had not harmed Muslims. Only those who did the Muslims wrong were to be chastised.

Just prior to the exodus from Mecca, some Meccans had issued a reward for Muhammad's assassination. Shortly afterwards a gang of young men forced their way into his house. Muhammad and Abu Bakr, a close friend, fled to the mountains outside of Mecca, where they hid in a cave. The attackers would have discovered them had not a rock dove and a spider contrived to conceal its entrance.

When Muhammad arrived safely in Medina, the Muslims there were overjoyed. It dawned on them that they had managed to break free of their tribe—the Quraysh—and had yet survived. Perhaps no other Arab peoples could make that claim. And because they ceased to be bound by ties of clan or tribe, theirs was a different type of community, one founded on faith (an *umma*).

But how should they govern themselves? Allah provided the answer:

Sura 7 (Allah Commands all Creation)

> **54.** **Your Lord is Allah, Who created the heavens and the earth in six days, then established Himself on the Throne. Truly, all creation are He commands All. Blessed be Allah, the Lord of the worlds.**

Other *suras* reinforce the point that Allah's dominion is exclusively under His control. Allah is the source of all authority on earth.

Before the Muslim migration to Medina, Arab and Jewish tribes had long contended for control of the town. Many of these Arabs welcomed the infusion of Muslim immigrants, assuming that the influx of well-disciplined Arabs would give them an advantage against the Jews of Medina. But Muhammad knew that the Quraysh tribes would attack the Muslim outpost in Medina. In order to defend the town, he sought to bring all of its inhabitants, including the Jewish tribes, into a Muslim-sponsored alliance. To that end, he instructed the Muslims to hold a special meeting every Friday afternoon, when Jews were preparing for the Sabbath; he also declared that Muslim men could marry Jewish women and eat Jewish food. Muhammad instructed Muslims to bow to Jerusalem during prayers, as did the Jews.

In short, Muhammad advised toleration with the "people of the Book"—Jews and Christians who had received the revelations of the Bible and who, like the Muslims, embraced monotheism.

As Muhammad became more familiar with the Jews of Medina, he perhaps appreciated the similarities of these two monotheistic religions. The *Book of Genesis*, moreover, included an intriguing detail that seemingly foreshadowed the origins of the Arab peoples. The crucial story came from the story of Abraham, the Jewish patriarch. According to *Genesis*, Abraham and Sarah had a son, Isaac; Abraham had another son, Ishmael, by his slave concubine Hagar. Sarah, favoring her own son, insisted that Abraham send Ishmael into the wilderness, where he became "an expert with a bow." The "wilderness," Muhammad concluded, referred to Arabia; and "an expert with a bow," referred to the nomadic Arabs. Ishmael, Abraham's son, was founder of the Arab nation. This revelation had momentous implications. If the Arab peoples were descended from Abraham, leader of the Jews, then the earliest Arabs believed in monotheism. Thus Islam did not constitute a repudiation of Arab traditions, but an affirmation of the core beliefs of the founders of the Arab nation. The *Qur'an* had rediscovered the lost Arab tradition of monotheism. Muhammad increasingly identified the Muslims as the descendants of Ishmael, and the nation of "Islam" as the "great nation," spawned in the "wilderness," as predicted in the Book of Genesis.

Sura 2, one of the most important, developed these and other points. It identified Allah as the same God worshipped by the "Children of Israel." Allah/God, though preferring the Jews "to all other nations," built the *Ka'aba* in Mecca as a house of worship for all mankind, consecrated by Abraham and Ishmael.

Word came from Mecca that an attack was imminent. Muhammad received a revelation outlining the rules governing Islamic warfare:

Sura 2 (Jihad: Do not Attack First, and Do Not Fight those who Surrender)

191. **Fight for the sake of Allah those that fight you. But do not attack them first. Allah does not love aggressors.**

192. **Slay *aggressors* wherever you find them. Drive them back! Idolatry is worse than bloodshed. But do not fight them within the precincts of the Holy Mosque unless they attack you there. If they attack you, put them to the sword. Thus shall the unbelievers be rewarded. Allah is forgiving, merciful.**

193. **Fight against them until idolatry has been extirpated.**

WAR WITH THE QURAYSH: VICTORY AT BADR, 624

But while the Muslims awaited attack from Mecca, they confronted another even more pressing problem. The Muslims who crowded into Medina were tradespeople; but Medina was a farming community whose arable land had already been occupied. The Muslims in Medina had no means of subsistence; how could the feed their families and house themselves? How could the Muslim *umma* hold together?

In 623, therefore, Muhammad authorized two raids against Mecca-bound caravans. Raids were not uncommon in Arabia: one needy tribe often seized the camels and goods of another, a practice that was tolerated as long as no one was hurt during the raids. But Arabian raiders never attacked their own tribe. The Muslims, in preying on the Meccan caravans, would be violating this principle. This was unprecedented.

The initial raids failed. But the Quraysh, outraged by these attacks, dispatched a 1000-man force to intercept the Muslim raiders. When the two armies converged in the desert near the village of Badr, the Meccans were routed, leaving fifty dead and seventy more prisoners. To nearly everyone's amazement, the Muslims had defeated the most powerful tribe in Arabia.

Such a victory, Muhammad revealed, could only have been achieved by Allah:

Sura 8 (Allah Slew the Unbelievers)

> 17. *You did not kill the Meccans; Allah slew them . . . Surely Allah is All-Hearing, All-Knowing.*

This victory confirmed Muhammad's belief that the Muslims were following in the footsteps of the ancient Jews: When the Jews were being oppressed by the Pharaohs and driven from their homes, God/Allah drowned the Egyptian army in the Red Sea. So, too, Allah had slain the Qurayshi oppressors. Believing that the Jews commemorated their deliverance from the Egyptian army at Passover, Muhammad called for an annual fast during Ramadan to commemorate the Muslim victory at Badr.[7]

STALEMATE BETWEEN MECCANS AND MUSLIMS: 625–627

But the war was not over. The Qurayshi leaders insisted that the Muslim victory at Badr had been a fluke; the Muslims could not withstand another such attack. Increasingly, too, Jewish tribes in Medina, alarmed at the swagger of the victorious Muslims, dispatched emissaries to Mecca: Medina, the Jews reported, was not united behind the Muslims; if the Meccans attacked again, many Jewish tribes there would support the attackers. Some Jewish tribes strengthened their own fortresses in Medina in expectation of a future showdown with the Muslims. The Meccans commenced plans for another offensive against Medina.

Early in 625, Muslim raiders seized another Qurayshi caravan. In March, the Quraysh sent some 3,000 men and as many camels—the cavalry—to attack Medina. Muhammad led some 1000 Muslim soldiers. The two armies converged about five miles from Medina, near a mountain at Uhud. As at Badr, the Quraysh initiated the attack with a cavalry charge; but this time the Muslims faltered. Muhammad tried to rally his men, but he was struck in the head and knocked unconscious. Many thought he was dead. But he regained consciousness and, by the end of the day, the Muslims regrouped. But 65 Muslim soldiers had been killed, against 22 Qurayshi soldiers. The Muslims had suffered a major defeat.

This posed serious theological problems. If Allah had slain the enemies of the Muslims at Badr, why did He not do so at Uhud? And if Muhammad truly was receiving Allah's guidance, why had the Muslim troops become confused? Why did they fail?

Several revelations answered these questions: In *Sura 3* Allah reiterated that Muhammad was merely a prophet: only Allah could win battles. And sometimes, Allah explained, He tested believers, all the better to discern who was worthy of Paradise.

---

7. Although the exact origins of Passover are uncertain, most sources agree that it celebrated the deliverance of the Jews from Egyptian bondage; but it probably was not a celebration of a military victory.

As the Muslim army limped back to Medina, Muhammad was forced to address problems caused by the defeat. Who would care for the wives and children of the soldiers who perished? In traditional Arab tribes, the extended clan provided sustenance and protection for all of its members. But the Muslims in Medina had severed their ties to the Quraysh tribe and their clans and kinfolk. They now were sustained by their Muslim community, the *umma*. But the *umma* lacked the structures to care for the new widows and their children. Muhammad's revelation addressed the problem:

Sura 4 (In Support of widows and orphans: in defense of polygamy)

2. *And give to the orphans the property (of their deceased parents), and take none of their property for yourself: to do so is a great crime.*

3. *And if you fear that you cannot act fairly towards orphans, then marry such women as seem good to you, perhaps two or even three or four; but if you fear that you cannot treat them equally, then only marry one or what your right hands possess [captives of war or slave-girls]; this is more proper, that you may not deviate from the right course.*

Muhammad himself took more wives, chiefly to build alliances with various Bedouin tribes.

During 626 the Quraysh and Muslims prepared for the decisive battle. In March 627, a Meccan army of some 10,000 men marched to Medina. The Muslims, augmented by Bedouin tribes, defended Medina with 3,000. To prepare for the Meccan onslaught, Muhammad ordered Muslims to dig a huge trench, mounding the excavated earth into a long defensive wall. When the Meccans arrived at the outskirts of Medina, they were stymied. They began a siege but eventually ran out of food and supplies and gave up, returning to Mecca. The Muslims had survived again, winning what became known as the Battle of the Trench.

After brief victory celebrations, the Muslims turned on one of the Jewish tribes in Medina that had betrayed them. The Muslims beheaded 700 men and sold the women and children into slavery.[8] A revelation explained:

Sura 33 (Destruction of the Jewish Traitors)

27. *Allah seized from their fortresses those who had supported the unbelievers from among the People of the Book [some of the Jews of Medina] and cast terror into their hearts: so you slew some of the Jews and took others captive.*

THE PILGRIMAGE TO MECCA AND VICTORY AGAINST THE MECCANS: 628–630

News of the failure of the big Meccan offensive and of the savage Muslim retaliation against the Jewish rebels reverberated throughout Arabia. Tribes increasingly regarded the Muslims as well-disciplined, well-motivated, and nearly invincible in battle. Many tribes that had been allied to the Meccans made new alliances with Muhammad. Muslim merchants established Medina as a trading center to rival Mecca. For their part, the Meccans also sensed that the tide had turned:

---

8. The massacre of one of the Jewish tribes of Medina, though an unspeakable barbarity, was not without precedent in the ancient world. To cite one example: According Hebrew Scriptures, Kind David slaughtered 200 Philistines, castrated them, and sent their foreskins to the Philistine King.

the failed offensive had exhausted their resources—and perhaps their will. Rather than attempt another attack, they waited for Muhammad and his allies to attack them in Mecca.

But now Muhammad changed directions. Allah had commanded Muhammad to undertake *jihad* not to crush the Quraysh, but to bring an end to idolatry: "Undertake *jihad* until idolatry shell cease and Allah's religion will be persecuted no more." Protracted war with the Quraysh could only weaken the Arabs and undermine Muhammad's larger cause. So rather than make plans for a crushing attack on Mecca, he sought an accommodation with the Quraysh. But how could he come to terms with those bent on destroying him and the Muslims?

In March 628, Allah revealed the solution:

Sura 48 (A pilgrimage to Mecca): 629

> 27. *Allah has fulfilled His Apostle's vision: "You shall enter the Sacred Mosque [of Mecca], as a religious pilgrim, safe and without fear, with your hair cropped or shaven. For Allah knew what you knew not; He ensured your swift victory."*

The morning after this revelation, Muhammad made an extraordinary announcement: at the behest of Allah, he would soon leave on a pilgrimage to the *Ka'aba* in Mecca. Other Muslims were free to join him, but none could carry weapons.

On hearing this, the Muslims' Bedouin allies rejected the pilgrimage as utter madness: the Quraysh would slaughter their Muslim enemies. Muhammad ignored all objections and made the necessary preparations. Allah had counseled war, and He had brought them victory; now He counseled tranquility—peace—and Muhammad proceeded without fear of the consequences.

Muhammad's purposefulness and confidence were infectious. When he finally set forth on his pilgrimage, he was joined by 1000 Muslims. All had shaved their heads and wore the white robes of traditional pilgrims.

The Quraysh were perplexed by the mass Muslim pilgrimage. Mecca had always ensured the right of pilgrims to enter Mecca and visit the *Ka'aba,* a guarantee that contributed to the ascendancy of Mecca as a trading center. But the Meccans were horrified by the prospect of Muhammad returning to Mecca in triumph, leading a procession of his fanatical followers. Some Qurayshi leaders proposed to intercept the Muslims and butcher them; others insisted that the Muslims be accorded the rights of all pilgrims. While the Meccans debated the matter, they sent a small army to the outskirts of Mecca to delay entry of the huge group of Muslim pilgrims, with Muhammad in the lead.

When forced to halt, the Muslims sat down in the desert. Then came the negotiations. Eventually Muhammad, perhaps infused with a sense of tranquility, accepted most of the terms proposed by the Quraysh. He agreed to end the pilgrimage and lead the Muslims back to Medina in return for a promise that Muslims would be granted admission to Mecca in all future years. Muhammad also promised to cease raiding Meccan caravans and to return future Muslim converts who fled to Medina. The Meccans accepted Muhammad's proposal to allow the Bedouin tribes to ally with either with Mecca or Medina. If both sides kept the treaty's provisions, a truce between Mecca and Medina would last for ten years.

When Muhammad announced the terms of the settlement to the pilgrims, they were appalled. How could they return to Medina without having completed their pilgrimage to Mecca? Opposition mounted when Muhammad ordered that converts who had escaped from Mecca be returned to the unbelievers in Mecca. Muhammad, some Muslims claimed, had betrayed the Muslim cause. Some considered mutiny. Never had Muhammad encountered such vehement internal opposition.

Then Muhammad announced, "A *sura* has descended upon me, which is dearer to me than anything under the sun."

Sura 48 (Allah's Tranquility Enfolds All Believers)

> **18. Allah was well-pleased with the believers; He knew what was in their hearts and sent down the Tranquility upon them and rewarded them with a victory near at hand"** . . .

This new "tranquility," or "serenity," as it is sometimes translated, marked a new approach to the situation in Arabia. The Bedouin tribes, free to ally with whichever side they preferred, increasingly sided with the Muslims.

By March of 629, moreover, the time for the agreed-upon Muslim pilgrimage to Mecca had come. Now nearly 3000 Muslims joined Muhammad. As the immense procession, wearing white garments, approached Mecca, the Quraysh evacuated the city. Muhammad led the pilgrims to the *Ka'aba,* the sacred black stone of antiquity, and he kissed it. An uncle who had opposed Muhammad now offered him his daughter in marriage; Muhammad invited the Quraysh, waiting in the nearby hills, to come to the wedding feast. After three days, as agreed, Muhammad led the pilgrims out of Mecca and back to Medina. The Quraysh watched in astonishment: the Muslims were disciplined, united, and joyous. Many Meccans converted on the spot.

THE TRIUMPH AT MECCA: 630

By early 630, Muhammad assembled a huge army and began a slow march towards Mecca. Most Qurayshi soldiers surrendered in advance of Muhammad's arrival and placed themselves under his protection. A few refused to give up. When the Muslims entered Mecca, a brief fight ensued; but the Muslim victory was swift. Muhammad ordered no reprisals and did not oblige the vanquished Meccans to accept Islam. Instead, he led a procession around the *Ka'aba* and shattered the 360 idols arrayed around the black stone, all the while intoning:

Sura 17 (The Truth has Come)

> **82. Say: "The Truth has Come, and falsehood has vanished; surely falsehood will vanish as well."**

As the Quraysh began to emerge from their houses, Muhammad called on them to join his *umma,* the great brotherhood of all Muslims (see Sura 49).

The practical benefits of "tranquility" became evident immediately: a week after the Meccan capitulation, only one tribe declared war on the Muslims; when Muhammad sent his army to meet them, it had been augmented by several thousand new Meccan converts. Another Muslim victory followed, and then others. In October of 630, Muhammad led an army in excess of 30,000 through vast stretches of Arabia, venturing north to the edge of the Byzantine Empire.

Whether his troops fought a battle at Tabouk is a source of debate, but the sweeping advance of the Muslim army introduced more Arab peoples to Islam. Tribalism and polytheism were fading before the Muslim onslaught.

As head of a huge army, Muhammad focused increasingly on military issues; new revelations further develop the concept of *jihad* (see Sura 9).

By early 631, nearly all of Arabia was under Muslim domination.

THE DEATH OF MUHAMMAD: 632

Muhammad had little time to enjoy the triumph of Islam. In 632, he made a farewell *hajj*, or pilgrimage, to Mecca. (Making such a pilgrimage subsequently became one of the duties enjoined on all Muslims, if at all possible.) On his return he complained of headaches and died shortly thereafter. Many Muslims responded with despair. But Abu Bakr, one of the first converts to Islam and a chief lieutenant of the Prophet, discouraged such displays of grief. He explained that Muhammad had insisted that he not become deified, as Christians had regarded Jesus. "O men, if anyone worships Muhammad, Muhammad is dead," Abu Bakr added. "If anyone worships Allah, Allah is alive, immortal."

THE LEGACY OF MUHAMMAD

Succession: Abu Bakr as Caliph

The Muslim *umma,* united during Muhammad's lifetime, became divided after his death. A council of prominent Muslims at Medina, claiming that Muhammad had named no successor, elected Abu Bakr as caliph, "successor" to the Prophet. But others insisted that Muhammad had named Ali, husband of Muhammad's daughter, Fatimah, as successor. Abu Bakr prevailed, but the dispute fractured the Muslim world—and does so to this day. Sunni Arabs, the dominant sect, adhere to the tradition established by Abu Bakr; Shi'ite Muslims, the major sect in Iran, regard Abu Bakr and his two successors as usurpers to a title that belonged to Ali, who, like all of Muhammad's family, benefited from divine inspiration.[9]

Bakr, as the first caliph, was forced to contend with two additional challenges: A host of would-be prophets surfaced; and some tribes that had been drawn into the Muslim orbit now sought to break away. Abu Bakr addressed both threats decisively: He proclaimed that Muhammad was the last of the prophets; anyone who claimed to be a prophet was an imposter and their revelations were fraudulent. And while Islam opposed coercion in matters of religion, no Muslim tribe that had accepted Allah now had the right to repudiate Him. Such willful denial of Allah warranted death. Abu Bakr's authority was complete.

---

9. In 656, after the assassination of the third caliph, Ali became the fourth caliph. His tumultuous reign was marked by civil war. He was assassinated in 661. His followers insisted that only Ali's male descendants were entitled to serve as caliph. Ali's son Husayn continued the struggle for control of the Muslims. In 680 he and his supporters were trapped and killed at Karbala in Iraq by troops of Mu'awiya I, founder of the Umayyad dynasty, who reigned as monarch-caliph.

The Spread of Islam

In 634 Abu Bakr died, but by then Islam had become an almost irresistible force: subsequent Islamic rulers did not supervise its expansion so much as channel its force in particular directions. Caliph 'Umar I, who ruled from 634–644, divided the world into two regions: one where Allah's will (Islam) prevailed (Dar al-Islam) and one where it did not (Dar al-Harb). Dar al-Islam was a realm of peace and justice; Dar al-Harb was a zone of war, into which Islam was to be projected. Like Abu Bakr, who worried that upstarts and usurpers would somehow seize Muhammad's message, 'Umar sought to suppress innovators—and innovations. To that end, he ordered the compilation of Muhammad's revelations into a single authoritative source—the *Qur'an;* he also ordered the destruction of all other collections of Muhammad's revelations.

The success of Muslim armies was partly due to vacuum caused by the decline of the Byzantine Empire and the earlier collapse of the Roman Empire. The Muslims conquered Damascus (Syria) in 637, Jerusalem in 638, Egypt in 642, and Persepolis (Iran) in 650. By the late 600s, Muslims had swept through most of northern Africa; in 711 they won victories throughout the Iberian Peninsula (now Spain and Portugal). Within a century of Muhammad's death, Islamic influence extended from the Atlantic Ocean to the frontier of India.

As they gained territory, wealth, and power, Muslim rulers were plagued by the schemes of rebellious generals and overlords, the revolts of subject peoples, as well as courtly intriguers and assassins—recurrent themes in the history of all ancient empires. Yet none of this halted the Muslim advance, nor sapped the movement of its Islamic message. Wherever Muslim armies triumphed, mosques were built,[10] local peoples converted to Islam, and the Arabic language and culture advanced. In the early years of conquest, Muslim rulers were sustained by the spoils of war; but increasingly they imposed taxes and initiated trade to generate revenue for the state. Jews and Christians ("People of the Book"), though allowed to practice their faiths, but were obliged to pay special taxes for that right.

The spread of Islam greatly exceeded the administrative capacity of the original rulers in Medina. By the tenth century, the Islamic empire had been fractured into a dozen separate realms ruled hereditary dynasties. In the early 1300s Osman I founded of the Ottoman Dynasty (modern Turkey). Over the next three-hundred years, Ottoman rulers succeeded in unifying the western portion of the Islamic empire and pushed northward far into Europe. Other major Islamic dynasties were located in India (Mughal Empire, 1526–1707) and Iran (Safavid Empire, 1501–1722).

Five Pillars of Islam

Islam demanded obedience; to that end, Muslim leaders propounded a simplified set of behavioral rules which by the late 600s became known as the Five Pillars of Islam:

> Witnessing to the oneness of Allah and the belief in Muhammad as Allah's final prophet; "There is no God but Allah and Muhammad is his Prophet." (*shahadad*)
> Performing the five prescribed prayers (*salat*) at daybreak, noon, mid-afternoon, sunset, and evening. The proper times are announced from the minaret of the mosque by the

---

10. In 692 the dome of the "Dome of the Rock" mosque in Jerusalem was completed; still standing, it is regarded as an exemplar of early Islamic architecture. In 715 the Great Mosque of Damascus was completed, built upon the ruins of the church of St. John.

muezzin (public announcer). This shows that one is a member of the community of believers (*Umma*).

Giving alms *(Zakah)* to the poor, for spreading the faith or for freeing debtors.

Observing of the month long fast of Ramadan, the ninth month of the lunar calendar. The believer refrains from eating, drinking water, and sexual activity during the daylight hours, sacrificing bodily desires for the sake of Allah.

Making at least one pilgrimage to Mecca, the most sacred of places, if at all possible.

In addition to these "Pillars," which are essentially practices, certain beliefs, held almost universally by Muslims, became normative. They included: belief in the Day of Judgment or the Last Day; Paradise as a reward for faithfulness; "jihad," or struggling for righteous in one's personal life and in society; just war in defense of the Islamic community against unbelievers; attitudes toward the place of women and children in society; sexuality as a God-given attribute to be properly enjoyed; the mark of a good ruler; martyrdom; free will and predestination.

Appendix C: Major Documents

WRITINGS OF KEY FIGURES IN SOUTH ASIA DURING THE LATE NINETEENTH AND TWENTIETH CENTURIES

HINDU REVIVAL

LEADERS OF THE INDIAN NATIONAL CONGRESS

B. R. AMBEDKAR AND THE UNTOUCHABLES

LEADERS OF THE MUSLIM LEAGUE

HINDU MAHASABHA

HINDU REVIVAL

Swami Vivekananda

Swami Vivekananda (1863–1902) was a key figure in promoting Hinduism as a major world religion, as indicated in the follow excerpts from his famous address to the World's Parliament of Religions at the Columbia Exposition of 1893 in Chicago. Although he insists that all religions fundamentally convey the same message, he particularly enshrines the message contained in the *Bhagavad Gita,* a sacred text of Hinduism: "Whosoever comes to Me, through whatsoever form, I reach him; all men are struggling through paths which in the end lead to Me." This phrase, and others which insist on Hinduism's capacity to absorb tenets from other faiths, says more about Hinduism than about those faiths. Vivekananda's impassioned defense of Hinduism helped nurture its revival during the late nineteenth century.

Advisory: Vivekananda's writings are especially useful to players who are writing about the deeply spiritual character of Indian peoples. "Hindus"—either within the INC or the Hindu Mahasabha—may borrow his arguments on the inclusive character of Hinduism; Muslim theorists may claim that Vivekananda's insistence that "all religions are true" reflects a Hindu sensibility rather than an Islamic one. Communists may cite Vivekananda to illustrate India's foolish reliance on religion, "the opiate of the masses."

"ADDRESSES AT THE PARLIAMENT OF RELIGION" (1893)

Sisters and Brothers of America, it fills my heart with joy unspeakable to rise in response to the warm and cordial welcome which you have given us. I thank you in the name of the most ancient order of monks in the world; I thank you in the name of the mother of religions; I thank you in the name of millions and millions of Hindu people of all classes and sects.

My thanks, also, to some of the speakers on this platform who, referring to the delegates from Orient, have told you that these men from far-off nations may well claim the honor of bearing to different lands the idea of toleration. I am proud to belong to a religion which has taught the world both tolerance and universal acceptance. **We believe not only in universal toleration,**

but we accept all religions as true. I am proud to belong to a nation which has sheltered the persecuted and the refugees of all religions and nations of the earth. I am proud to tell you that we have gathered in our bosom the purest remnant of the Israelites, who came to Southern India and took refuge with us in the very year in which their holy temple was shattered to pieces by Roman tyranny. I am proud to belong to the religion which has sheltered and is still fostering the remnant of the grand Zoroastrian nation. I will quote to you, brethren, a few lines from a hymn which I remember to have repeated from my earliest boyhood, which is every day repeated by millions of human beings: 'As the different streams having their sources in different places all mingle their water in the sea, sources in different tendencies, various though they appear, crooked or straight, all lead to Thee.'

The present convention, which is one of the most august assemblies ever held, is in itself a vindication, a declaration to the world of the wonderful doctrine preached in the *Gita*: 'Whosoever comes to Me, through whatsoever form, I reach him; all men are struggling through paths which in the end lead to Me.' Sectarianism, bigotry, and its horrible descendant, fanaticism, have long possessed this beautiful earth. They have filled the earth with violence, drenched it often and often with human blood, destroyed civilization and sent whole nations to despair. Had it not been for these horrible demons, human society would be far more advanced than it is now . . .

Much has been said of the common ground of religious unity. I am not going just now to venture my own theory. But if anyone here hopes that this unity will come by the triumph of any one of the religions and the destruction of others, to him I say, 'Brother, yours is an impossible hope.' Do I wish that the Christian would become Hindu? God forbid. Do I wish that the Hindu or Buddhist would become Christian? God forbid.

The seed is put in the ground, and earth and air and water are placed around it. Does the seed become the earth, or the air, or the water? No. It becomes a plant, it develops after the law of its own growth, assimilates the air, the earth, and the water, converts them into plant substance, and grows into a plant.

Similar is the case with religion. The Christian is not to become a Hindu or a Buddhist, nor a Hindu or a Buddhist to become a Christian. But each must assimilate the spirit of the others and yet preserve his individuality and grow according to his own law of growth.

If the Parliament of Religions has shown anything to the world it is this: It has proved to the world that holiness, purity and charity are not the exclusive possessions of any church in the world, and that every system has produced men and women of the most exalted character. In the face of this evidence, if anybody dreams of the exclusive survival of his own religion and the destruction of the others, I pity him from the bottom of my heart, and point out to him that upon the banner of every religion will soon be written, in spite of resistance: 'Help and not Fight,' 'Assimilation and not Destruction,' 'Harmony and Peace and not Dissension'.

From: John Henry Burrows, ed., The World's Parliament of Religions: An Illustrated and Popular Story of the World's First Parliament of Religions, Held in Chicago in Connection with the Columbian Exposition of 1893 (Chicago: The Parliament Publishing Company, 1893).

Bal Gangadhar Tilak

B. G. Tilak (1856–1920), the son of Brahmans, was an ardent proponent of Indian independence. He learned English and Sanskrit from his father, a schoolteacher, and received both an undergraduate degree and a law degree. But unlike so many others, Tilak eschewed a career in the British bureaucracy and instead went into journalism, publishing a newspaper (in the dialect of Marathi) that won a large audience among Hindus in the Maharashtra. He promoted festivals honoring the Maratha warrior, Shivaji. After the assassination of several British officials in 1897, Tilak was sentenced to jail for inciting violence. He was among the most popular of the Hindu radicals in the INC.

Advisory: Hindu extremists may wish to focus on Tilak's enshrinement of Shivaji, the Hindu warrior; Muslims may regard Tilak's writings as proof of the incompatibility of Hindus and Muslims within India. Secularists within the INC and the Muslim League may cite Tilak's extremism as justification for excluding religion from politics. But everyone should be mindful that Tilak's views won wide acceptance among Hindu villagers.

"Is Shivaji Not a National Hero?" (1906)

Hero-worship is a feeling deeply implanted in human nature; and our political aspirations need all the strength which the worship of a Swadeshi hero is likely to inspire within our minds. For this purpose Shivaji is the only hero to be found in the Indian history. He was born at a time when the whole nation required relief from misrule; and by his self-sacrifice and courage he proved to the world that India was not a country forsaken by Providence. It is true that the Mahomedans [Muslims] and the Hindus were then divided; and Shivaji who respected the religious-scruples of the Mahomedans, had to fight against the Mogul [Muslim dynasty] rule that had become unbearable to the people. But it does not follow from this that, now that the Mahomedans and the Hindus are equally shorn of the power they once possessed and are governed by the same laws and rules, they should not agree to accept as a hero one who in his own days took a bold stand against the tyranny of his time.

It is not preached nor is it to be at all expected that the methods adopted by Shivaji should be adopted by the present generation. The charge brought by the Anglo-Indian writers [those Indians who were educated in British schools and universities] in this connection is a fiction of their own brain and is put forward simply to frighten away the timid amongst us. No one ever dreams that every incident in Shivaji's life is to be copied by any one at present. **It is the spirit which actuated Shivaji in his doings that is held forth as the proper ideal to be kept constantly in view by the rising generation.** No amount of misrepresentation can succeed in shutting out this view of the question from our vision; and we hope and trust that our Mahomedan friends will not be misled by such wily methods. We do not think that the Anglo-Indian writers will object to England worshipping [Admiral] Nelson or France worshipping the great Napoleon on the ground that such national festivals would alienate the sympathies of either nation from the other, or would make the existence of amicable relations between the two nations an impossibility in the future. The Shivaji festival is not celebrated to alienate or even to irritate, the Mahomedans.

Times are changed, and, as observed above, the Mahomedans and the Hindus stand in the same boat or on the same platform so far as the political condition of the people is concerned. Can we not both of us derive some inspiration from the life of Shivaji under these circumstances? That is the real question at issue . . . We are not against a festival being started in honor of Akbar [the great sixteenth-century Muslim emperor of the Mughal dynasty] or any other hero from old Indian history. But that of Shivaji has a peculiar value of its own for the whole country, and it is the duty of every one to see that this characteristic of the festival is not ignored or misrepresented. Every hero, be he Indian or European, acts according to the spirit of his times; and we must therefore judge of his individual acts by the standard prevalent in his time. If this principle be accepted we can find nothing in Shivaji's life to which one can take exception. But as stated above we need not go so far. What makes Shivaji a national hero for the present is the spirit which actuated him and not his deeds as such. His life clearly shows that Indian races do not so soon lose the vitality which gives them able leaders at critical times. That is the lesson which the Mahomedans and the Hindus have to learn from the history of the great Marratta chief; and the Shivaji festival is intended to emphasize the same lesson.

From *B. G. Tilak: His Writings and Speeches* (Madras: Ganesh & Co., 1918).

Rabindranath Tagore

Rabindranath Tagore (1861–1941) was a major figure in poetry, winner of the Nobel Prize in literature in 1913, the first non-European to win that coveted prize. His poetry was written in Bengali. If Swami Vivekananda helped popularize Hinduism and cement its importance within world religions, Tagore established the importance of Indian literature. Tagore did not show that Indians could write as well as Europeans and Americans, but that they wrote **differently.** His especially showed the distinct power and message of Indian writing. The excerpt below describes the educational mission Tagore established and supported. It also reflects his belief that Hinduism, with its ties to nature and the rhythms of existence, is an antidote to modernity—a pivotal theme in Gandhi's writings as well.

Advisory: Tagore's writings indicate his opposition to British educational patterns. His own school—Visva-Bharati—seeks to cultivate the soulfulness of every individual. Unlike so many British-educated Indians, Tagore sees no reason why Indians should aspire to European-style education—or modernity and "progress." Europeans, in promoting economic growth and materialism, have neglected that which matters most: man's spirituality. This essay can buttress Gandhian thoughts, and also the thinking of most Hindus. Muslims may argue that Tagore's insistence on the fundamental spirituality of all men ignores the deep differences separating Hindus and Muslims. Economic materialists and Communists may deride Tagore as hopelessly backward, his emphasis on man's spirituality nothing more than an "opiate" to mask the misery of the impoverished masses.

"THE EDUCATIONAL MISSION OF VISVA-BHARATI," THE MODERN REVIEW (JUNE, 1931)

I have been asked to speak this evening to my invisible audience about the educational mission to which I have devoted my life and I am thankful for this opportunity.

. . . [W]hen I was young I underwent the mechanical pressure of a teaching process, one of man's most cruel, and most wasteful mistakes . . . At the age of twelve I was first coerced into learning English. Most of you in this country are blissfully unconscious of the mercilessness of your own language. You will admit, however, that neither its spelling, nor its syntax, is perfectly rational. The penalty for this I had to pay, without having done anything to deserve it, with the exception of being born ignorant.

When in the evening my English teacher used to come I was dragged to my daily doom at a most unsympathetic desk and an unprepossessing textbook containing lessons that are followed by rows of separated syllables with accent-marks like soldiers' bayonets.

As for that teacher, I can never forgive him. He was so inordinately conscientious! He insisted on coming every single evening, there never seemed to be either illness or death in his family. He was so preposterously punctual too. I remember how the fascination for the frightful attracted me every evening to the terrace facing the road; and just at the right moment, his fateful umbrella—for bad weather never prevented him from coming—would appear at the bend of our lane.

Remembering the experience of my young days, of the schoolmasters and the classrooms, also knowing something of the natural school which nature herself supplies to all her creatures, I established my institution in a beautiful spot, far away from the town, where the children had the greatest freedom possible under the shade of ancient trees and the field around open to the verge of horizon.

From the beginning I tried to create an atmosphere which I considered to be more important than the class teaching. The atmosphere of nature's own beauty was there waiting for us from a time immemorial with her varied gifts of colors and dance, flowers and fruits, with the joy of her mornings and the peace of her starry nights. I wrote songs to suit the different seasons, to celebrate the coming of spring and the resonant season of the rains following the pitiless months of summer. When nature herself sends her message we ought to acknowledge its compelling invitation . . .

From the commencement of our work we have encouraged our children to be of service to our neighbors from which has grown up a village reconstruction work in our neighborhood unique in the whole of India. Round our educational work the villages have grouped themselves in which the sympathy for nature and service for man have become one. In such extension of sympathy and service our mind realizes its true freedom.

Along with this has grown an aspiration for even a higher freedom, a freedom from all racial and national prejudice . . . **We are building up our institution upon the ideal of the spiritual unity of all races.** I hope it is going to be a great meeting place for individuals from all countries who believe in the divine humanity, and who wish to make atonement for the cruel disloyalty displayed against her by men. Such idealists I have frequently met in my travels in the West, often unknown persons, of no special reputation, who suffer and struggle for a cause generally ignored by the clever and the powerful.

For some time past, education has lacked idealism in its mere exercise of an intellect which has no depth of sentiment. The one desire produced in the heart of the students has been an ambition to win success in the world, not to reach some inner standard of perfection, not to obtain self-emancipation . . .

I have this one satisfaction that I am at least able to put before you the mission to which these last years of my life have been devoted. As a servant of the great cause I must be frank and strong in urging upon you this mission. I represent in my [educational] institution an ideal of brotherhood where men of different countries and different languages can come together. I believe in the spiritual unity of man, and therefore I ask you to accept this task from me . . .

I believe that the social unrest prevalent today all over the world is owing to the anarchy of spirit in the modern civilization. What is called **progress** is the progress in the mechanical contrivances; it is in fact an indefinite extension of our physical limbs and organs which, owing to the enormous material advantage that it brings to us, **has tempted the modern man away from his inner realm of spiritual values.** The attainment of perfection in human relationship through the help of religion, and cultivation of our social qualities occupied the most important place in our civilization up till now. But today our homes have dissolved into hotels, community life is stifled in the dense and dusty atmosphere of the office, men and women are afraid of life, people clamour for their rights and forget their obligations, and they value comfort more than happiness and the spirit of display more than that of beauty.

Great civilizations in the East as well as in the West have flourished in the past because they produced food for the spirit of man for all time; they tried to build their life upon the faith in ideals, the faith which is creative. These great civilizations were at last run to death by men of the type of our precocious schoolboys of modern times, smart and superficially critical, worshippers of self, shrewd bargainers in the market of profit and power, efficient in their handling of the ephemeral, who presume to buy human souls with their money and throw them into their dustbins by suicidal forces of passion, set their neighbors' houses on fire and are themselves enveloped by the flame.

It is some great ideal which creates great societies of men; it is some blind passion which breaks them to pieces. They thrive so long as they produce food for life; they perish when they burn up life in insatiate self-gratification. We have been taught by our sages that it is truth and not things which saves man from annihilation.

The reward of truth is peace, the reward of truth is happiness. The people suffer from the upsetting of equilibrium when power is there and no inner truth to which it is related, like a motor care in motion whose driver is absent.

From Rabindranath Tagore, *The Modern Review* (June 1931).

Lala Lajpat Rai

Lajpat Rai (1865–1928) was taught by his father, a Hindu. At 16 he attended the Punjab University College in Lahore. He swiftly passed the necessary legal exams and practiced law, first as a clerk. He promoted Hindu culture and, by the 1890s, became a prominent proponent of Hindu nationalism in the Punjab. His anti-British political activities in 1907 caused him to be deported to Burma for six months. When he returned to India he called for work stoppages (*hartals*) and other means of passive resistance, anticipating the techniques of Gandhi. In 1925 he became an official of the Hindu Mahasabha, a new organization promoting Hindu extremism.

Advisory: Supporters of Hindu extremism (within the INC and the Hindu Mahasabha) may cite Lajpat Rai's writings, as would opponents of Hindu extremism, including secularists within the INC (Nehru) and most members of the Muslim League.

"SWADESHI" (INDEPENDENCE)

India was [once] said to be only a geographical expression. It has now begun to aspire, under the guidance of an All-Wise Providence to a unified political existence, and to a place in the comity of nations. The congeries of nations that are said to inhabit this vast territory have, after a long period of disunion and disorganization, begun to realize that, after all, **they are one people with one common blood running through their veins, with common traditions, common history and a common faith in their future.** It is true that communities are divided from communities, sects from sects, and Provinces from Provinces, by differences of religion, language and customs. The wave of Western civilization, however, with its unifying influence, is leveling down these differences and creating a community of interest and feeling which is the precursor of a new dawn in our life. Some time ago, people began to look back and find that with all their differences, they were, after all, the **branches of a common tree,** the descendants of the same stock, the inheritors of the same civilization, with local differences only. Practically they were speakers of the same language. Even Mahomedans [Muslims], taken as a whole, could not say that in their traditions, languages and customs, they had nothing in common with the Hindus. This looking backwards made them compare their present position with the position of their people in other parts of the world, and led them to look forward. Thus was awakened the national consciousness which, for want of greater occasions, has begun to exhibit itself in demonstrations and ovations in honor of individuals, who have even by slight sacrifices earned the distinction of being the servants of the country. Interpreting these ovations in this sense, I feel I have every reason to rejoice over them.

From *The Indian Nation Builders, Part I* (Madras: Ganesh & Co., Madras, 1918), 336–45.

LEADERS OF THE INDIAN NATIONAL CONGRESS

Gandhi

Mohandas Gandhi (1869–1948), a Hindu, was born into the merchant caste within the Gujarat region of India. He acquired a law degree in London and a first became known as *Mahatma* ("high-souled") for his work on behalf of blacks and Indians in South Africa in 1914. He returned to India the next year, and soon became a leader of the independence movement and president (in 1921) of the Indian National Congress. His basic political program is outlined in "My Position" (1925) below, namely, his attempts to broker a political alliance between Hindus and Muslims; his desire to bring an end to Untouchability; and his opposition to modernity (and consequently his enthusiasm for traditional artisanal trades, such as spinning cloth). Other essays in this section elaborate on these points, such as his conception of passive resistance as a confrontational tactic; and his conviction that the *Bhagavad Gita,* a classic Hindu text, can serve as a guide for political action in the modern world. A final essay—"Caste and Outcaste"—shows that while Gandhi disapproves of the mistreatment of Untouchables, he retains faith in the four castes within the Hindu system.

Advisory: Muslims may emphasize the "Hindu" aspects of Gandhi's thought, as proof that Gandhian India would be hostile to Muslims. The leaders of the Hindu Mahasabha may also underscore such texts, as proof that modern India must remain true to its Hindu roots. Secularists within the INC and the Muslim League, and the Communists may attack many of the views presented here. Dr. Ambedkar, a leader of the Untouchables, may cite the strongly Hindu character of Gandhi's writings, partly in support for Ambedkar's breaking away and seeking his own direction forward. Nehru and the Hindu Mahasabha may be appalled by the "Wardha" system of education, which emphasizes simple crafts, such as spinning. Gandhi has little interest in creating a strong nation state or promoting economic growth.

"MY POSITION" (1925)

Let me make my position clear. I am wedded to the **three-fold program.**

(1) **I cannot tease Hindu-Muslim Unity into life.** It therefore requires no outward activity from me. As a Hindu I shall serve as many Musalmans [Muslims] as will let me serve them. I shall advise those who seek my advice. For the rest, I cease to worry about what I cannot mend. But I have a living faith in unity coming. It must come even if it has to do so after a few pitched battles. If there are men who will fight, nobody on earth can prevent them.

(2) **Untouchability is doomed.** It may take time. But the progress made is truly marvelous. It is more still in the thought world. But in action too one notices the effect everywhere. It was a glorious sight, the other day, to see in Mangrol [a small city in the Gujarat region of India, near Gandhi's home] not one of the [Hindu] ladies raising her hand against untouchables sitting side by side with them. And when [the untouchables] were actually brought in none of these brave women moved. It is not a solitary instance. But I know that there is a dark side to the picture. Hindus must unremittingly toil away at the reform. The larger the number of workers, the more substantial the result.

(3) But the most encouraging results are to be seen in spinning. **[Spinning] is spreading to the villages.** I make bold to say that it is the most effective method of village reconstruction. There are thousands of women hungering to spin, because they want a few coppers to find them food . . . There are millions in India who have lost all interest in life. We can only touch them by ourselves spinning. I am interested in producing the spinning atmosphere. When many people do a particular thing, it produces a subtle unperceivable effect which pervades the surroundings and which proves infectious. I want that atmosphere so that the idle hands I have described will be irresistibly drawn to the wheel. They will be so drawn when they see people spinning who do not need to. Hence the franchise . . . Organization for non-violence means giving villagers remunerative work to do and inducing them to give up some of their bad habits and to bring into being consciousness of one nationality by making untouchables proud of their Hinduism and bringing Hindus, Musalmans and others to believe in and to work for the common cause with a full heart. I have no aptitude for any other work along political lines till the three things are done.

From *Young India* (April 16, 1925).

"War vs. Non-Violence" (1921)

My business is to refrain from doing any violence myself, and to induce by persuasion and service as many of god's creatures as I can to join me in the belief and practice. But I would be untrue to my faith, if I refused to assist in a just cause any men or measures that did not entirely coincide with the principle of non-violence. I would be promoting violence, if finding the Mussalmans to be in the right, I did not assist them by means strictly nonviolent against those who had treacherously plotted the destruction of the dignity of Islam. Even when both parties believe in violence there is often such a thing as justice on one side or the other. A robbed man has justice on his side, even though he may be accounted as a triumph of non-violence, if the injured party could be persuaded to regain his property by methods of *satyagraha* (love or soul-force) rather than a free fight.

From *Young India* (January 6, 1921).

"Doctrine of the Sword" (1920)

I do believe that, where there is only a choice between cowardice and violence, I would advise violence. Thus when my eldest son asked me what he should have done, had he been present when I was almost fatally assaulted in 1908, whether he should have run away and seen me killed or whether he should have used his physical force which he could and wanted to use, and defended me, I told him that it was his duty to defend me even by using violence. Hence it was that I took part in the Boer War, the so-called Zulu rebellion and the late War. Hence also do I advocate training in arms for those who believe in the method of violence. I would rather have India resort to arms in order to defend her honor than that she should in a cowardly manner become or remain a helpless witness to her own dishonor.

But I believe that non-violence is infinitely superior to violence, forgiveness is more manly than punishment. Forgiveness adorns a soldier. But abstinence is forgiveness only when there is the power to punish; it is meaningless when it pretends to proceed from a helpless creature. A mouse hardly forgives a cat when it allows itself to be torn to pieces by her. I therefore appreciate the sentiment of those who cry out for the condign punishment of General Dyer [British commander who ordered the massacre at Amritsar in 1919] and his ilk. They would tear him to pieces if they could. But I do not believe India to be helpless. I do not believe myself to be a helpless creature. Only I want to use India's and my strength for a better purpose.

Let me not be misunderstood. Strength does not come from physical capacity. It comes from an indomitable will. An average Zulu [a tribe in South Africa] is any way more than a match for an average Englishman in bodily capacity. But he flees from an English boy, because he fears the boy's revolver or those who will use it for him. He fears death and is nerveless in spite of his burly figure. We in India may in a moment realize that one hundred thousand Englishmen need not frighten three hundred million human beings. A definite forgiveness would therefore mean a definite recognition of our strength. With enlightened forgiveness must come a mighty wave of strength in us, which would make it impossible for a Dyer to heap affront upon India's devoted head. It matters little to me that for the moment I do not drive my point home. We feel too downtrodden not to be angry and revengeful. But I must not refrain from saying that India can gain more by waiving the right of punishment. We have better work to do, a better mission to deliver to the world.

I am not a visionary. I claim to be a practical idealist. The religion of non-violence is not meant merely for the Rishis [sages of ancient Hindu texts] and saints. It is meant for the common people as well. Non-violence is the law of our species as violence is the law of the brute. The spirit lies dormant in the brute and he knows no law but that of physical might. The dignity of man requires obedience to a higher law—to the strength of the spirit.

I have therefore ventured to place before India the ancient law of self-sacrifice. For Satyagraha and its off-shoots, Non-co-operation and civil resistance, are nothing but new names for the law of suffering. The Rishis, who discovered the law of non-violence in the midst of violence, were greater geniuses than Newton. They were themselves greater warriors than Wellington [the British general who defeated Napoleon]. Having themselves known the use of arms, they realized their uselessness and taught a weary world that its salvation lay not through violence but through non-violence.

Non-violence in its dynamic condition means conscious suffering. It does not mean meek submission to the will of the evildoer, but it means the putting of one's soul against the will of the tyrant. Working under this law of our being, it is possible for a single individual to defy the whole might of an unjust empire to save his honor, his religion, his soul and lay the foundation for that empire's fall or its regeneration.

And so I am not pleading for India to practice non-violence, because it is weak. I want her to practice non-violence being conscious of her strength and power. No training in arms is required for realization of her strength. We seem to need it, because we seem to think that we are but a lump of flesh. I want India to recognize that she has a soul that cannot perish and that can rise triumphant above every physical weakness and defy the physical combination of a whole world.

[But] I invite even the school of violence to give this peaceful non-cooperation a trial. It will not fail through its inherent weakness. It may fail because of poverty of response. Then will be the time for real danger. The high-souled men, who are unable to suffer national humiliation any longer, will want to vent their wrath. They will take to violence. So far as I know, they must perish without delivering themselves or their country from the wrong. If India takes up the doctrine of the sword, she may gain momentary victory.

Then India will cease to be [the] pride of my heart. I am wedded to India, because I owe my all to her. I believe absolutely that she has a mission for the world. She is not to copy Europe blindly. India's acceptance of the doctrine of the sword will be the hour of my trial. I hope I shall not be found wanting. My religion has no geographical limits. If I have a living faith in it, it will transcend my love for India herself. My life is dedicated to service of India through the religion of non-violence which I believe to be the root of Hinduism.

From *Young India* (August 11, 1920).

"Non-violence and the Bhagavad Gita" (1925)

I have room in my philosophy of life for *Kshatriyas* [warrior caste]. But my definition of him I take from the *[Bhagavad] Gita*. He who does not run away from battle, *i.e.* danger, is a *Kshatriya*. As the world progresses the same terms acquire new values . . . If a large number of people carry out the doctrine of non-resistance, the present state of the world will not be what it is. Those individuals who have carried it out have not lost anything. They have not been butchered by the violent and the wicked. On the contrary the latter have shed both their violence and wickedness in the presence of the non-violent and the good.

I have already stated my meaning of the *Gita*. It deals with the eternal duel between good and evil. And who does not, like Arjuna, often quail when the dividing line between good and evil is thin and when the right choice is so difficult?

I heartily endorse, however, the statement that he alone is truly non-violent who remains non-violent even though he has the ability to strike. I do therefore claim that my disciple (I have only one and that is myself) is quite capable of striking, very indifferently and perhaps ineffectively I admit; but he has no desire to do so. I have had in my life many an opportunity of shooting my opponents and earning the crown of martyrdom but I had not the heart to shoot any of them. For I did not want them to shoot me, however, much they disliked my methods. I wanted them to convince me of my error as I was trying to convince them of theirs. 'Do unto others as you would that they should do unto you.'

From *Young India* (May 7, 1925).

"The Wardha Scheme of Education" (1937)

I am convinced that the present system of primary education [under auspices of the British government] is not only wasteful, but is positively harmful. Most of the boys are lost to their parents and to the occupation [to which] they are born. They pick up evil habits, affect the urban ways, get a smattering of something which may be anything but education. What then should be the form of primary education? I think the remedy lies in educating them by means of vocational or manual training . . .

[T]he scheme that I wish to place before you today is not the teaching of some handicrafts side by side with liberal education. **I want that the whole education should be imparted through some handicraft and industry.** Teaching of *takli* spinning, for instance, presupposes the imparting of knowledge of the various varieties of cotton, different soils in different provinces of India, history of the ruin of handicraft, its political reasons, which will include the history of British rule in India, knowledge of arithmetic and so on. I am trying the same experiment on my grandson, who scarcely feels that he is being taught, for he all the while plays, laughs and sings. I am especially mentioning the *takli* and emphasizing its utility because I have realized its power and its romance; also because the handicraft of making cloth is the only one which can be taught throughout the country and because the *takli* is very cheap . . . I have contemplated a seven years' course which so far as *takli* is concerned would culminate in practical knowledge of weaving, including dyeing, designing, etc.

I am very keen on funding the expenses of a teacher through the product of the manual work of his pupils, because I am convinced that there is no other way to carry education to *crores* of our children. [a crore is a numbering system used in Hindi, Urdu, Bengali and other South Asian languages: one crore = 10 million]. We cannot wait until we have the necessary revenue and until the [British] viceroy reduces the military expenditure. You should bear in mind that this primary education would include the elementary principles of sanitation, hygiene, nutrition, of doing their own work, helping parents at home, etc. The present generation of boys knows no cleanliness, no self-help, and are physically weak. I would, therefore, give compulsory physical training through the musical drill.

I have been accused of being opposed to literary training. Far from it, I simply want to show the way in which it should be given. The self-supporting aspect has also been attacked. It is said, whereas we should be expending millions on the primary education, we are going to exploit the children. [But] **whilst the child will be encouraged to spin and help his parents with agricultural jobs, he will also be made to feel that he does not belong only to his parents but also to the village and to the country, and that he must make some return to them. That is the only way. I would tell the ministers that they would make the children helpless by doling out education to them. They would make them self-confident and brave by their paying for their own education by their own labor.** The system is to be common to all Hindus, Muslims, Parsis and Christians. Why do I not lay any religious instructions, people ask. Because I am teaching them practical religion, the religion of self-help.

College education was largely an urban proposition. I would not say that it was an unmitigated failure, as primary education was, but the results were fairly disappointing. Why should anyone of the graduates have to be unemployed?

We have to make our boys true representatives of our culture and our civilization, of the true genius of our nation. We cannot do so otherwise than by giving them a course of self-supporting primary education.

From *Harijan* (July 31, 1937).

"FROM CART AND CHARKHA" (1925)

[A friend] asked whether I propose to replace the railways with country carts, and if I did not, how I expected to replace mills with wheels. I told him that I did not propose to replace railways with carts because I could not do so even if I wished. Three hundred million carts could not destroy distance. **But I could replace mills with [spinning] wheels.** For railways solved the question of speed. With mills it was a question of production in which the wheel could easily compete if there were enough hands to work as there were in India. I told him that as a matter of fact a villager could manufacture for himself sufficient cloth cheaper than mills if he did not count the value of his labor. And he did not need to do so as he would spin or even weave during his spare hours. It is remarkable how false or incomplete analogies deceive people. In the case in point, the difference between mills and railways on the one hand and wheels and country-carts on the other, is so obvious that the comparison should never have been made. But probably the friend thought I was against all machinery in every conceivable circumstance. Probably he had in mind my objections to railways stated in my *Indian Home Rule* though I have repeatedly said that I am not working out the different fundamental problems raised in that booklet.

From *Young India* (May 28, 1925).

"CASTE AND OUTCASTE" (1933)

It is a wrong to destroy caste because of the outcaste, as it would be to destroy a body because of an ugly growth in it or of a crop because of the weeds. The outcasteness, in the sense we understand it, has therefore to be destroyed altogether. It is an excess to be removed, if the whole system is not to perish. Untouchability is the product, therefore, not of the caste system, but of the distinction of high and low that has crept into Hinduism and is corroding it. The attack on untouchability is thus an attack upon this 'high-and-low'-ness. The moment untouchability goes, the caste system itself will be purified, that is to say, according to my dream, it will resolve itself into the true Varnadharma, the four division of society, each complementary of the other and none inferior or superior to any other, each as necessary for the whole body of Hinduism as any other.

From Harijan (November 2, 1933).

Jawaharlal Nehru

Born in Allahabad, Nehru (1889–1964), the son of a wealthy lawyer, was educated at home by English tutors. At fifteen, he was sent to England, where he received an undergraduate degree from Cambridge University and a law degree from the Inns at Court in London. In 1912, he returned to India, working for his lawyer father, who was also an increasingly prominent figure in the Indian National Congress. Nehru became a follower of Gandhi, and went to jail for his political activities in 1920. But where Gandhi focused on Indian spirituality and opposed (European) modernity, Nehru increasingly embraced European socialism and even communist doctrines. His opposition to capitalism was intensified by the Great Depression, which seemingly confirmed Marx's prediction that capitalism would lead to overproduction, underemployment, wars of imperialism and economic collapse. With Gandhi's support, Nehru was elected president of the Indian National Congress from 1930–1934. He was elected several other times within the next decade. Unlike Gandhi, who insisted that India needed no armed forces, Nehru believes that India must have a strong central government—including sufficient armed forces to protect the emerging nation.

Advisory: Indian Communists can cite Nehru's criticism of capitalism and his support of socialism and communism as endorsements of their own programs; similarly, secularists within the INC can also cite Nehru's proposal to de-emphasize religious issues. The Hindu Mahasabha can try to lure Nehru to their side—he does support a strong central government and defense; though the Hindu Mahasabha's explicit Hinduism is seemingly incompatible with Nehru's secularism. Gandhi and other Hindus may try to push Nehru away from his support for "European" state socialism.

For copyright reasons, Nehru's texts should be consulted online. Conduct a web search for Nehru's "Presidential Address to the INC at Lahore" (1929), "Whither India" (1933; see "This is the crisis of capitalism" through "making you happy"), and "Marxism, Capitalism, and India's Future" (1941).

B. R. AMBEDKAR AND THE UNTOUCHABLES

B. R. Ambedkar (1891–1956) was a leader of the Untouchables. Though he was born into an Untouchable family, his father, who worked for the British army, insisted that his children learn to read the Hindu classics. Ambedkar was the only untouchable to attend the local government school; he was obliged to sit outside the room on a gunny sack, and listen to the lessons inside. He was the only Untouchable to attend the high school and, ultimately, its affiliated college, the College of Bombay. Upon graduation he attained advanced degrees in London and New York (including a PhD in economics at Columbia University).

Advisory: In the following essay, Ambedkar adopts a risky strategy. He endorses swaraj—Indian independence—although he concedes that the Hindu majority may be more repressive than the British. But he notes that 150 years of British rule had done little to improve the lives of Untouchables. Ambedkar then insists that the only way the Untouchables lives will be improved is if they gain some measure of political power. He also regards Hindu majorities at the provincial level as the key obstacle to political power for Untouchables. Thus he wants a strong central Indian government, with full political participation of the Untouchables. Other minorities, such as the Muslims and Sikhs, may endorse Ambedkar's strategy, if only to weaken the political power of Hindus in the central government. The Hindu Mahasabha may find much to support in Ambedkar's program; the Muslims may wish to promote antagonism between Ambedkar and the INC.

"THE DEPRESSED CLASSES" (1932)

Mr. Chairman. My purpose in rising to address this Conference is principally to place before it the point of view of the depressed classes, whom I . . . have the honor to represent, regarding question of constitutional reform. It is a point of view of 43,000,000 people, or one-fifth of the total population of British India. The depressed classes form a group by themselves which is distinct and separated from the Muhammadans [Muslims], and, although they are included among the Hindus, they in no sense form an integral part of that community. Not only have they a separate existence, but they have also assigned to them a status which is invidiously distinct from the status occupied by any other community in India . . .

That point of view I will try to put as briefly as I can. It is this: that the bureaucratic form of government in India should be replaced by a government which will be a government of the people, by the people and for the people . . . The depressed classes welcomed the British as their deliverers from age-long tyranny and oppression by the orthodox Hindus. They fought their battles against the Hindus, the Mussalmans [Muslims] and the Sikhs, and won for them this great Empire of India. The British, on their side, assumed the role of trustees for the depressed classes. [But] when we compare our present position with the one which it was our lot to bear in Indian society of the pre-British days, we find that, instead of marching on, we are only marking time.

Before the British, we were in the loathsome condition due to our untouchability. Has the British government done anything to remove it? Before the British, we could not draw water from the village well. Has the British Government secured us the right to the well? Before the British, we could not enter the temple. Can we enter now? Before the British, we were denied entry into the Police Force. Does the British Government admit us in the Force? Before the British, we were not allowed to serve in the Military. Is that career now open to us? To none of these questions can we give an affirmative answer. That the British, who have held so large a sway over us for such a long time, have done some good we cheerfully acknowledge. But there is certainly no fundamental change in our position. Indeed, so far as we are concerned, the British Government has accepted the social arrangements as it found them . . . Our wrongs have remained as open sores and they have not been righted, although 150 years of British rule have rolled away . . .

This is therefore the inevitable conclusion which the depressed classes have come to: namely, that the bureaucratic Government of India, with the best of motives, will remain powerless to effect any change so far as our particular grievances are concerned. We feel that nobody can remove our grievances as well as we can, and we cannot remove them unless we get political power in our own hands. No share of this political power can evidently come to us so long as the British Government remains as it is. It is only in a Swaraj [independence] constitution that we stand any chance of getting the political power into our own hands, without which we cannot bring salvation to our people.

There is one point with which I should like to deal before I close this matter. We are often reminded that the problem of the depressed classes is a social problem and that its solution lies elsewhere than in politics. We take strong exception to this view. We hold that **the problem of the depressed classes will never be solved unless they get political power in their own hands.** If this is true, and I do not think that the contrary can be maintained, then problem of depressed classes is I submit eminently a political problem and must be treated as such. We know that political power is passing from the British into the hands of those who wield such tremendous economic, social and religious sway over our existence. We are willing that it may happen, though the idea of Swaraj recalls to the mind of many of us the tyrannies, oppressions and injustices practiced upon us in the past and fear of their recurrence under Swaraj. We are prepared to take the inevitable risk of the situation in the hope that we shall be installed, in adequate proportion, as the political sovereign of the country along with our fellow countrymen. But we will consent to that on one condition and that is that the settlement of our problems is not left to time. I am afraid the depressed classes have waited too long for time to work its miracle . . .

The settlement of our problem must be a part of the general political settlement and must not be left over to the shifting sands of the sympathy and goodwill of the rulers of the future. The reasons why the depressed classes insist upon it are obvious. Every one of us knows that the man in possession is more powerful than the man who is out of possession. Every one of us also knows that those in possession of power seldom abdicate in favour of those who are out of it. We cannot therefore hope for the effectuation of the settlement of our social problem, if we allow power to slip into the hands of those who stand to lose by settlement unless we are to have another revolution to dethrone those whom we today help to ascend the throne of power and prestige. We prefer being despised for too anxious apprehensions, than ruined by too confident a security, and I think it would be just and proper for us to insist that the best guarantee for the settlement of our problem is the adjustment of the political machine itself so as to give us a hold on it, and not the will of those who are contriving to be left in unfettered control of that machine.

What adjustments of the political machine the depressed classes want for their safety and protection I will place before the Conference at the proper time. All I will say at the present moment is that, although we want responsible government, we do not want a Government that will only mean a change of masters. Let the Legislature be fully and really representative if your Executive is going to be fully responsible.

I am sorry Mr. President I had to speak in such plain words. But I saw no help. The depressed classes have had no friend. The government has all along used them only as an excuse for its continued existence. The Hindus claim them only to deny them or, better still, to appropriate, their rights. The Muhammedans [Muslims] refuse to recognise their separate existence, because they fear that their privileges may be curtailed by the admission of a rival. Depressed by the government, suppressed by the Hindu and disregarded by the Muslim, we are left in a most intolerable position of utter helplessness to which I am sure there is no parallel and to which I was bound to call attention.

Regarding the other question which is set down for discussion I am sorry it was decided to tag it on to a general debate. Its importance deserved a Session for itself. No justice can be done to it in a passing reference. The subject is one in which the depressed classes are deeply concerned and they regard it as a very vital question. As members of a minority, we look to the Central Government to act as a powerful curb on the provincial majority to save the minorities from the misrule of the majority. As an Indian interested in the growth of Indian nationalism, I must make it plain that I am a strong believer in the unitary form of Government and the thought of disturbing it I must confess does not please me very much. This unitary government has been the most potent influence in the building up of the Indian nation. That process of unification which has been the result of a unified system of Government has not been completed and I should be loathed to withdraw this most powerful stimulus in the formative period and before it has worked out its end. However, the question, in the form in which it is placed, is only an academic question and I shall be prepared to consider a federal form, if it can be shown that in it local autonomy is not inconsistent with central unity.

Sir, all that I, as a representative of the depressed classes, need say on their behalf I have said. May I crave your indulgence to permit me as an Indian to say a word or two generally on the situation, which we have to meet. So much has been said regarding its gravity that I shall not venture to add a word more to it, although I am no silent spectator of the movement. What I am anxious about is to feel whether we are proceeding on right lines in evolving our solution. What that solution should be rests entirely upon the view that British Delegates choose to take. Addressing myself to them I will say, whether you will meet the situation by conciliation or by applying the iron heel must be a matter for your judgement—for the responsibility is entirely yours . . .

I am afraid it is not sufficiently realized that in the present temper of the country, no constitution will be workable which is not acceptable to the majority of the people. The time when you were to choose and India was to accept is gone, never to return. Let the consent of the people and not the accident of logic be the touchstone of your new constitution, if you desire that it should be worked.

From the Official Report of the Second Round Table Conference, 1932 (Calcutta: Government of India, Central Publication Branch, 1932).

LEADERS OF THE MUSLIM LEAGUE

Muhammad Iqbal

Born in the Punjab, Iqbal (1873–1938) was raised by pious parents who taught him the *Qur'an,* the sacred text of the Muslims. He graduated from the Government College (Lahore) in 1899 and then taught philosophy there. After studying at Cambridge University, he returned to teaching in Lahore in 1908. Rather than continue to work for the British government, he worked as a lawyer in private practice. But most of his energies were devoted to writing. He became perhaps the world's greatest Urdu poet and one of its finest Islamic thinkers. Unlike many Muslim thinkers, Iqbal insisted that Muslims must be actively involved in politics. But his notion of a modern state was imbued with Islamic principles.

Advisory: The following essay can be used in support of Muslim independence. And also against a Muslim political state. Iqbal's ardent religious convictions can be challenged by other players, including Jinnah, the secularist within the League. Hindus can cite Iqbal as proof that India must be divided into Muslim and Hindu states.

1932 PRESIDENTIAL ADDRESS TO THE ALL INDIA MUSLIM CONFERENCE

. . . Politics have their roots in the spiritual life of man. It is my belief that Islam is not a matter of private opinion. It is a society, or, if you like, a civic church. It is because present-day political ideals, as they appear to be shaping themselves in India, may affect its original structure and character that I find myself interested in politics. I am opposed to nationalism as it is understood in Europe, not because, if it is allowed to develop in India, it is likely to bring less material gain to Muslims. I am opposed to it because I see in it the germs of atheistic materialism which I look upon as the greatest danger to modern humanity. Patriotism is a perfectly natural virtue and has a place in the moral life of man. **Yet that which really matters is a man's faith, his culture, his historical tradition. These are the things which, in my eyes, are worth living for and dying for,** and not the piece of earth with which the spirit of man happens to be temporarily associated. In view of the visible and invisible points of contact between the various communities of India, I do believe in the possibility of constructing a harmonious whole whose unity cannot be disturbed by the rich diversity which it must carry within its bosom . . .

The present struggle in India is sometimes described as India's revolt against the West. I do not think it is a revolt against the West; for the people of India are demanding the very institutions which the West stands for. Whether the gamble of elections, retinues of party leaders and hollow pageants of parliaments will suit a country of peasants to whom the money-economy of modern democracy is absolutely incomprehensible, is a different question altogether. Educated urban India demands democracy. The minorities, feeling themselves as distinct cultural units and fearing that their very existence is at stake, demand safeguards which the majority community [Hindus], for obvious reasons, refuses to concede. The majority community pretends to believe in a nationalism, theoretically correct, if we start from Western premises, belied by facts, if we look to India. Thus the real parties to the present struggle in India are not England and India, but the majority community and the minorities of India [Muslims, Sikhs, Untouchables] which can ill afford to accept the principle of Western democracy until it is properly modified to suit the actual conditions of life in India.

Nor do Mahatma Gandhi's political methods signify a revolt in the psychological sense.

These methods arise out of a contact of two opposing types of world-consciousness, Western and Eastern. The Western man's mental texture is chronological in character. He lives and moves and has his being in time. The Eastern man's world-consciousness is non-historical. To the Western man things gradually become; they have a past, present and future. To the Eastern man they are immediately rounded off, timeless, purely present. That is why Islam which sees in the time-movement a symbol of reality appeared as an intruder in the static world-pictures of Asia. The British as a Western people cannot but conceive political reform in India as a systematic process of gradual evolution. Mahatma Gandhi as an Eastern man sees in this attitude nothing more than an ill-conceived unwillingness to part with power and tries all sorts of destructive negations to achieve immediate attainment. Both are elementally incapable of understanding each other. The result is the appearance of a revolt.

. . . Our ideal is well defined. It is to win in the coming constitution a position for Islam which may bring her opportunities to fulfill her destiny in this country. ...What then shall be our future program? I am inclined to think that it should be partly political, partly cultural. I venture to offer a few suggestions for your consideration.

[Iqbal proceeds to outline the need for a nationwide Muslim organization and for Muslim cultural organizations to educate young Muslims as well as Islamic political and legal institutions.]

Apart from the purely practical value of this proposal for the Muslims of India, we must remember that the modern world, both Muslim and non-Muslim, has yet to discover the infinite value of the legal literature of Islam and its significance for a capitalistic world whose ethical standards have long abdicated from the control of man's economic conduct. The formation of the kind of assembly I propose will, I am sure, bring a deeper understanding of the usual principles of Islam at least in this country.

From *The Eastern Times* (March 21, 1932).

Muhammad Ali Jinnah

Muhammad Ali Jinnah (1876–1948) was born in Karachi, the son of a Muslim trader. Like Gandhi and Iqbal, Jinnah was educated in London. When his father had several reverses in business, Jinnah returned to India (1896) and in 1903 practiced law in Bombay, where he became wealthy. In 1913 Jinnah joined the Muslim League and tried to unify the ML and the INC. This failed. In 1931 he withdrew from politics and focused on his legal practice. Muslim candidates fared poorly in the 1935 elections. In 1940, however, Jinnah endorsed Iqbal's call for a separate Muslim state.

Advisory: Jinnah's position within the Muslim League is roughly comparable to that of Nehru's within the INC. But this makes Jinnah a potential ally of Nehru, and vice versa. The INC will rebut many of the arguments continued within Jinnah's "Presidential Address," though the Hindu Mahasabha—and Gandhi—may find much to agree with.

PRESIDENTIAL ADDRESS TO THE ALL INDIA MUSLIM LEAGUE (1940)

"India's Problem of Her Future Constitution"

A leading journal like the *London Times*, commenting on the Government of India Act of 1935, wrote, 'undoubtedly the difference between the Hindus and Muslims is not of religion in the strict sense of the word but also of law and culture, that they may be said indeed to represent two entirely distinct and separate civilizations. However, in the course of time these superstitions will die out and India will be moulded into a single nation.' So according to the *London Times* the only difficulties are superstitions. These fundamental and deep-rooted differences, spiritual, economic, cultural, social and political have been euphemized as mere 'superstitions.' But surely, it is a flagrant disregard of the past history of the sub-continent of India as well as the fundamental Islamic conception of society *vis-à-vis* that of Hinduism to characterize them as mere 'superstitions.' Notwithstanding thousand years of close contact, nationalities which are as divergent today as ever, cannot at any time be expected to transform themselves into one nation merely by means of subjecting them to a democratic constitution and holding them forcibly together by unnatural and artificial methods of British Parliamentary Statutes . . .

If the British Government are really in earnest and sincere to secure peace and happiness of the people of this sub-continent, the only course open to us all is to allow the major nations separate homelands by dividing India into 'autonomous national states' [India and Pakistan]. There is no reason why these states should be antagonistic to each other. On the other hand the rivalry and the natural desire and efforts on the part of one to dominate the social order and establish political supremacy over the other in the government of the country will disappear. It will lead more towards natural good will by international pacts between them, and they can live in complete harmony with their neighbors. This will lead further to a friendly settlement all the more easily with regard to minorities by reciprocal arrangements and adjustments between Muslim India and Hindu India, which will far more adequately and effectively safeguard the rights and interests of Muslim and various other minorities.

It is extremely difficult to appreciate why our Hindu friends fail to understand the real nature of Islam and Hinduism. They are not religions in the strict sense of the word, but are, in fact, different and distinct social orders and it is a dream that the Hindus and Muslims can ever evolve a common nationality, and this misconception of one Indian nation has gone far beyond the limits and is the cause of more of our troubles and will lead India to destruction if we fail to revise our notions in time. The Hindus and Muslims belong to two different religious philosophies, social customs, literature. They neither intermarry, nor [dine] together and, indeed they belong to two different civilizations which are based mainly on conflicting ideas and conceptions. Their aspects on life and of life are different. It is quite clear that Hindus and Mussalmans [Muslims] derive their inspiration from different sources of history. They have different epics, their heroes are different, and different episodes. Very often the hero of one is a foe of the other and, likewise their victories and defeats overlap. **To yoke together two such nations under a single state, one as a numerical minority and the other as a majority, must lead to growing discontent and final destruction** of any fabric that may be so built up for the government of such a state.

History has presented to us many examples, such as the Union of Great Britain and Ireland, Czechoslovakia and Poland. History has also shown to us many geographical tracts, much smaller than the sub-continent of India, which otherwise might have been called one country but which have been divided into as many states as there are nations inhabiting them. Balkan Peninsula comprises as many as seven or eight sovereign states. Likewise, the Portuguese and the Spanish stand divided in the Iberian Peninsula. Whereas under the plea of unity of India and one nation, which does not exist, it is sought to pursue here the line of one central government when, we know that the history of the last twelve-hundred years, has failed to achieve unity and has witnessed, during the ages, India always divided into Hindu India and Muslim India . . .

Muslim India cannot accept any constitution which must necessarily result in a Hindu majority government. Hindus and Muslims brought together under a democratic system forced upon the minorities can only mean Hindu Raj. Democracy of the kind with which the Congress High Command is enamoured would mean the complete destruction of what is most precious in

Islam. We have had ample experience of the working of the provincial constitutions during the last two and a half years and any repetition of such a government must lead to civil war and raising of private armies as recommended by Mr. Gandhi to Hindus of Sukkur [a city within Sindh, a province with a Muslim majority] when he said that they must defend themselves violently or non-violently, blow for blow, and if they could not they must emigrate.

Mussalmans [Muslims] are not a minority as it is commonly known and understood. One has only got to look round. Even today according to the British map of India, out of eleven provinces, where the Muslims dominate more or less, are functioning notwithstanding the decision of the Hindu Congress High Command to non-co-operate and prepare for civil disobedience. Mussalmans are a nation according to any definition of a nation and they must have their homelands, their territory and their state. We wish to live in peace and harmony with our neighbors as a free and independent people. We wish our people to develop to the fullest our spiritual, cultural, economic, social and political life in a way that we think best and in consonance with our own ideals and according to the genius of our people. Honesty demands and vital interest of millions of our people impose a sacred duty upon us to find an honorable and peaceful solution, which would be just and fair to all. But at the same time we cannot be moved or diverted from our purpose and objective by threats or intimidations. We must be prepared to face all difficulties and consequences, make all the sacrifices that may be required of us to achieve the goal we have set in front of us.

From *The Eastern Times (*March 25, 1940); also Government of Pakistan website: Chronology (last accessed July 24, 2013).

HINDU MAHASABHA

Vinayak Savarkar

Vinayak Savarkar (1883–1966), born a Brahman from Maharashtra province, Savarkar sought to drive the British from India—and simultaneously assert the formidable power of India. He studied in London from 1906–1910, and learned details of radical strategy, including revolutionary violence. His "New India" group learned how to make Molotov cocktails—improvised explosive devices using large cans of gasoline. Savarkar also completed *The First Indian War of Independence of 1857,* a history text celebrating Indian independence, and bemoaning its current weakness. Savarkar was implicated in a successful assassination of a British official; Savarkar was sent to a prison camp in the Andaman Islands. He was released in 1924; he returned to India to campaign for Indian independence.

Advisory: Secularists within the INC and Muslim League can cite Savarkar's extreme views. The Communist Party may wish to endorse the same approach. The Muslim League can cite Savarkar as a main reason why they are wary of an alliance with Hindus.

HINDUTVA: WHO IS A HINDU? (1923)

. . . [N]o people in the world can more justly claim to get recognized as a racial unit than the Hindus and perhaps the Jews. A Hindu marrying a Hindu may lose his caste but not his *Hindutva* [Hindu culture]. A Hindu believing in any theoretical or philosophical or social system, orthodox or heterodox, provided it is unquestionably indigenous and founded by a Hindu may lose his sect but not his Hindutva—his Hindu-ness—because the most important essential which determines it is the inheritance of the Hindu blood . . .

. . . a moment's consideration would show that [these] two qualifications of one nation and one race—of a common fatherland and therefore of a common blood—cannot exhaust all the requisites of *Hindutva*. The majority of the Indian Mohammedans [Muslims] may, if free from the prejudices born of ignorance, come to love our land as their fatherland, as the patriotic and noble-minded amongst them have always been doing. The story of their conversions, forcible in millions of cases, is too recent to make them forget, even if they like to do so, that they inherit Hindu blood in their veins. But can we, who here are concerned with investigating into facts as they are and not as they should be, recognize these Mohammedans as Hindus? Many a Mohammedan community in Kashmir and other parts of India as well as the Christians in South India observe our caste rules to such an extent as to marry generally within the pale [region of settlement] of their castes alone; yet, it is clear that though their original Hindu blood is thus almost unaffected by an alien adulteration, yet they cannot be called Hindus in the sense in which the term is actually understood, because, **we Hindus are bound together not only by the tie of love . . . but also by that of a common culture.**

We have tried to make it clear that Hindutva is not to be determined by any theological tests. Yet we must repeat it once more that the Sikhs are free to reject any or all things they dislike as Sanatandharma [ancient Hinduism, as interpreted by Hindus sympathetic to the political revival of Hinduism in the late nineteenth century], even the binding authority of the *Vedas* as a revelation. They thereby may cease to be Sanatanis, but cannot cease to be Hindus. Sikhs are Hindus in the sense of our definition of *Hindutva* and not in any religious sense whatever. Religiously they are Sikhs as Jains are Jains, Lingayats are Lingayats, Vaishnavas are Vaishnavas. But all of us racially and nationally and culturally are a polity and a people, one and indivisible, most fitly and from times immemorial called Hindus. No other word can express our racial oneness . . .

Another reason besides this fear of being indentified [sic] as with the followers of Sanatanpanth which added to the zeal of some of our Sikh brothers and made them insist on getting classes separately as non-Hindus, was a political one. This is not the place of entering into merits or demerits of special representation. The Sikhs were naturally anxious to guard the special interests of their community and if the Mohammedans could enjoy the privilege of a special and communal representation, we do not understand why any other important minority in India should not claim similar concession. But we feel that, that claim should not have been backed up by our Sikh brothers by an untenable and suicidal plea of being non-Hindus. Sikhs, to guard their own interests could have pressed for and succeeded in securing special and communal representation on the ground of being an important minority as our non-Brahmins and other communities have done without renouncing their birthright of Hindutva.

Will they disown their seed, forswear their fathers and sell their birthright for a mess of pottage? God forbid! Let our minorities remember that if strength lies in union, then in Hindutva lies the firmest and yet the dearest bond that can effect a real, lasting and powerful union of our people. You may fancy that it pays you to remain aloof for the passing hour, but it would do incalculable harm to this our ancient race and civilization as a whole –and especially to yourselves. Your interests are indissolubly bound with the interests of your other Hindu brethren. Whenever in the future as in the past a foreigner raises a sword against the Hindu civilization it is sure to strike you as deadly as any other Hindu community. Whenever in future as in the past the Hindus as a people come to their own and under a Shivaji or a Ranjit, a Ramchandra or a Dharma, an Ashoka or an Amoghwarsha feeling the quickening touch of life and activity mount the pinnacles of glory and greatness—that day would shed its lustre on you as well as on any other members of our Hindu commonwealth. So, brothers, be not lured by the immediate gains, partly or otherwise, nor be duped by misreadings and misinterpretations of history . . .

From Vinayak Damodar Savarkar, *Hindutva: Who is a Hindu?* (Bombay: S. S. Savarkar, 1923).

Appendix D: Suggested Readings

For a fresh (though lengthy) introduction to Hinduism, see Wendy Doniger, *The Hindus: An Alternative History* (2009). On Islamic influence see Richard Eaton, *The Rise of Islam and the Bengal Frontier, 1204–1760* (1993), and Francis Robinson, *Islam and Muslim History in South Asia* (2000). See also John S. Hawley and Vasudha Narayanam, *The Life of Hinduism* (2006).

An excellent account of the collapse of the Mughal Empire is Muzaffar Alam, *The Crisis of Empire in Mughal North India, 1707–1748* (1986). On the origins of the Sikhs, see J. S. Grewal, *The Sikhs in the Punjab* (1990). The rise of the Maratha Empire is chronicled in Stewart Gordon, *The Marathas: 1600–1818* (1993). On the East India Company, see Ridhika Singha, *A Despotism of Law* (1998). The 1857 revolution is examined in Eric Stokes, *The Peasant Armed* (1986), and Radrangshu Mukherjee, *Awadh in Revolt* (1984).

B R. Tomlinson provides a useful survey of economic policies and developments in *The Economy of Modern India, 1860-1970* (1993). An older but still valuable account of founders of the Indian nation is Anil Seal, *The Emergence of Indian Nationalism* (1968). See also Stanley Wolpert, *Tilak and Gokhale* (1962), and Barbara D. Metcalf, *Islamic Revival in British India: Deoband, 1860–1900* (1982). See also Ainslie Embree, *India's Search for National Identity* (1972).

Students of Gandhi should begin with his autobiography, *My Experiments with Truth* (1957). For a recent, Pulitzer Prize–winning biography of Gandhi, see Joseph Lelyveld, *Great Soul: Mahatma Gandhi and His Struggle with India* (2011). Other works include Judith Brown, *Gandhi and Civil Disobedience, 1928–1934* (1977).

Ayesha Jalal, *The Sole Spokesman: Jinnah, the Muslim League and the Demand for Pakistan* (1985) offers a revisionist interpretation of the founder of Pakistan. For more on Nehru, see Judith M. Brown, *Nehru: A Poltical Life* (2003).

The rise of militant Hinduism is examined in Christophe Jaffrelot, *The Hindu Nationalist Movement and Indian Politics* (1996). On the response of the Indian princely states to the changing situation, see Ian Copland, *The Princes of India in the Endgame of Empire, 1917–1947* (1997).

For an up-to-date account of partition and its aftermath, see Yasmin Khan, *The Great Partition: The Making of India and Pakistan* (2007).

Acknowledgments

We wish to thank the following instructors who provided feedback on the game and the "Unfinished Journey" section. Their thoughtful comments were central to strengthening and clarifying the account of the events, peoples, and figures framing the Simla conference of 1945.

Amber Abbas, St. Joseph's University
Rashmi Chilka, Northern Virginia Community College
Kerry Dobbins, McPherson College
Ian McNeely, University of Oregon
Charles Reed, Elizabeth City State University
Penelope Sinanoglou, Wake Forest University
Paul Teverow, Missouri Southern State University
Judith Walden, *Simpson College*

CPSIA information can be obtained
at www.ICGtesting.com
Printed in the USA
LVHW042103091222
734911LV00004B/421